Let's Eat

Let's Eat

Recipes from My Kitchen Notebook

Tom Parker Bowles

St. Martin's Press ≋ New York

For Freddy

www.stmartins.com

Production manager: Adriana Coada

ISBN 978-1-250-01433-7

First U.S. Edition: October 2012

10 9 8 7 6 5 4 3 2 1

{ Contents }

Introduction

I have a battered old leather recipe book, dark blue and stained with fat, ketchup, and chilli sauce. And this book provides most of the recipes for *Let's Eat*. Entry into this shabby journal is every bit as exacting as a stage with Thomas Keller or Marco Pierre White. Each recipe has to earn its place. The process goes as follows: I travel to Mexico City, Bangkok, Palermo, Bolton, or Vientiane. And eat. Everywhere and everything, my belly swelling as the days go past.

I take copious, scrawled notes and jot down recipes on scraps of paper, everything from ticket stubs to napkins (and as anyone who has ever spent any time eating Asian street food knows, their napkins make loo rolls seem like canvas). Once back at my desk in London I attempt to decipher the name of a dish hiding beneath an errant scrap of noodle. Or a local ingredient blurred by a dousing of beer.

Yet this is not simply a traveller's tome, but a collection of very British recipes, too. The food I grew up eating, and still adore. The shepherd's pies and grilled sole, fresh asparagus and roasted grouse that never cease to thrill and delight.

At home, I cook each recipe at least three times, endlessly amending until it works (and gets the seal of approval from my wife; seriously, when she nods, the whole world agrees). Then, and only then, is it transcribed into the book. As the years pass, comments and additions find their way onto the pages. I love this leather volume, as much as I love my much-abused wok. Both have the patina of time and constant use, dirty and ragged to the outsider, but utterly beautiful to me. This book, like the wok, tells the story of my love of food. The scribbled additions, the infantile representations of the perfect-size meatball, and the scrawled notes, illegible to anyone but myself.

This book, like the wok, tells the story of my love of food. The scribbled additions, the infantile representations of the perfect-sized meatball and the scrawled notes, illegible to anyone but myself

Let's Eat doesn't set out to sharpen your
knife skills, nor redefine
the way you view food
Taste takes precedence over
pretty presentation and I've
little time for dreary finger-
wagging.

Let's Eat doesn't set out to sharpen your
knife skills, nor redefine the way you view
food. Taste takes precedence over pretty
presentation and I've little time for pious
finger-wagging. Buy the best you can afford.
Good free-range meat does cost more. The
animals take longer to grow, are killed later,
and are hung (in the case of beef) often for
longer than a month. This means extra cash,
sure. As well as extra flavour. And an immeasurably happier life for those beasts, too. But
having promised I wouldn't, I'm starting to
lecture from the lofty heights of my food
writer's ivory tower.

The same goes for those endlessly
repeated mantras of seasonal and local. Of
course seasonal food is important, as this
quarterly demarcation brings changes to the
market and kitchen that never cease to
delight. I passionately believe that the first
British asparagus, arriving in late spring, is
worth hanging on for, the taste made all the
better by the nine-month wait, served with
good melted butter and a sprinkling of salt.
The same goes for grouse in August, native
oysters in September (one drop of Tabasco,
one of lemon), gull's eggs in May, and straw-
berries in June. As one ingredient shuffles off
for another year, it's replaced by something
equally beguiling. But I can't bear those
boorish types who scream bloody murder if
you eat an apple in spring.

I'm all for local food, too, but don't start
quivering with rage at the thought of air-
freighted fruits and fancies. Our diet would
be pretty dull without the likes of lemons and
pepper, chocolate and coffee, rice and fish
sauce. And is it really so evil to prefer a
glossy, firm onion grown a hundred miles
away to some rotten, squidgy specimen from
that crap shop down the road? Pragmatism is
the key, not po-faced gloom.

Too often, cookbooks are written by chefs
who've long forgotten the constraints of the
home kitchen. I promise that there'll be no
recipe starting with the instruction, "Take 30
litres of veal stock . . ." or "Dip the whole pine
nuts into the pine nut praline and then dip
them into the liquid nitrogen . . ." Most of us

hardly have room for a mini blender, let alone a Pacojet processor or *sous-vide* bath.

Over the years, I've cooked every recipe in this book in my own kitchens. Some of them were no bigger than the average store-cupboard. If you can soften onions on the wonky electric ring of a canary yellow Baby Belling with only two settings—searing and Hades—then you can do anything.

For me, cooking is so much more than the application of heat to ingredients. It makes me happy; from the planning and shopping to the preparation and eating. With the radio trilling away in the background and a glass of wine at my right hand, I feel as if all is well in the world: cooking as catharsis, as ritual, as bliss. Plus there's the ironically selfish pleasure that cooking for others can bring: friends and family all gathered around the table. "Why is it that young couples buy a television or sofa before a table?" is a question that vexes chef Fergus Henderson. And quite rightly so.

Food is not just mere "lifestyle." It's our one shared universal experience. You can be celibate, teetotal, and tax-dodging, but you still have to eat. It's the basis of all economies, the catalyst for wars, and the keeper of peace. The move from hunter-gatherer to sedentary farmer saw the birth of civilization as we know it. And the history of a country, of its invasions and conquests, is far better illustrated through the food we eat than through some dusty, desiccated historical tome.

Food, too, is the great communicator. My grasp of foreign tongues is shaky, to say the least. Yet the symbol of enjoyment, the rubbing of one's gut, is universal. One gets to see far more of an alien culture from behind a robata grill, zinc bar, or home-made smoker than from any number of insipid guidebooks.

All the dishes in this book are within easy reach of anyone who can turn on an oven and grasp a knife. I'm a resolutely amateur cook, my culinary education untainted by years spent in restaurant kitchens. I'm messy and bumbling, with presentation generally more suited to Bedlam than Bocuse. These, though, are recipes to make the taste buds grin and the belly cheer.

Let's Eat takes the choicest cuts from ten years spent as a professional food writer, and throws it into one volume. I've banged on enough. Let's eat.

{ Comfort food }

"Landlord, bring us beans and bacon,
and a bottle of your finest Burgundy."

G. K. Chesterton

If beans, bacon, and Burgundy don't ooze comfort, then God only knows what does. Comfort food is familiar, without fuss, drama, or pomp. Straightforward, reliable, and ever welcome, this is the Ronseal of recipe types: "Does exactly what it says on the tin." It's all about easy pleasure and solid flavours, an edible balm that tastes exactly as it should.

It is, though, the most subjective of culinary categories, as the choice of dish is defined entirely by one's gastronomic past. A childhood spent tugging the apron strings of a great English cook will produce markedly different dishes to a youth passed alongside wok and cleaver. Yet anyone with a heartbeat and opposable thumb will have at least one dish—be it hot buttered toast, red lentil dhal, or peppered tripe soup—that coddles, comforts, and soothes.

The majority of dishes here are European in genesis, as comfort food is particularly well suited to temperate climes; a later chapter deals with food from far-off lands, too. There's a good sprinkling of British food. These are the staple dishes of my youth, adolescence, and adult life. A week will rarely pass when I don't cook at least one of these recipes. Bonhomie for the belly and succor for the soul.

{ Cooking at home }

"Heat is just another form of seasoning," I was once told by that Celtic force of nature, chef Richard Corrigan. This is a man whose intelligence is matched only by his generosity and, as ever, he's spot on. The flavour and texture of a piece of meat is affected by the amount of heat used, from quick sear to slow simmer. Yet too often the amateur cook fears real heat. We soften our onions on a piddling flame, and complain that it takes thirty minutes, not ten. We're afraid of burning our meat, rather than browning it. And we struggle with gas that seems to have only two settings: nothing and too hot.

Experience is everything, and the more that I cook and learn, the easier things become. I still panic at the thought of hollandaise sauce, for example, yet soufflés hold no fear. It doesn't help when chefs tell us how easy everything is, forgetting that they can bone chickens in their sleep, whereas I'd rather braise my own nose than attempt it again.

Professional chefs do have many advantages: when they dry-fry chillies, they have extractor fans that are so powerful they rip the words straight from their lips. No question of gassing out the house as it does at home. Nor do they have to contend with the smell of burnt dripping hanging around the sitting room for weeks after cooking huge portions of boeuf Bourguignon. Or the stench of french fry fat clinging tenaciously to every fiber. They can blacken steaks to their hearts' content, flambé duck without fear of ruining the ceiling, and fling the fat with reckless abandon. That is the point of a professional kitchen.

At home, things must be a little more subdued, but it's never quite as calm as the blessed Delia Smith might suggest. She makes it look easy, as she's been doing what she does, beautifully, for many years. All I'm saying is that cooking is often messy, smelly, noisy, and painful. That a pan full of hot fat will always spit like a cobra when introduced to a handful of raw meat. And sharp knives continue to slice open even the most lauded of hands. Don't fear the heat, and cooking suddenly becomes a whole lot easier.

{ Fat }

Once upon a time, in the not-so-distant past, we worshipped fat. Fat was health, wealth, and happiness. "The fat of the land" was something to be coveted rather than disdained. We hankered after great wobbling dollops of marrow, gleaned from the bone with a specially shaped scoop. Fought over the last scrap of chicken skin. And lusted after lard, dripping, suet, schmaltz, and butter. Fat carries flavour and aroma, provides the sexiest of textures, allows us to relish in our meat and delight in our food. Without fat, life would be one long lunch with Hare Krishnas.

Fat is also utterly essential to human life: our brains wouldn't function without the stuff, our cells would cease to survive. Hormones would wither and die, immune systems would buckle.

If the body were allowed to choose its fuel, it would go for fat, no question. Fat provides double the energy of similar amounts of protein and carbohydrates. Yet fifty years back, saturated fat suffered a spectacular fall from grace: from hero to zero in a matter of months. Scientists noted that coronary heart disease had suddenly become the biggest killer of all. At the same time, after the bleak paucity of the rationing years, there was an increased consumption of animal fats. No surprises there. Fourteen years of mock goose and Woolton pie will do that to an appetite. Scientists put two and two together and came up with four and a half. More animal fats, more heart disease, ergo animal fat is a gimlet-eyed, stone-cold killer. Animal fats became Public Enemy Number One. Despite the fact that there has been no conclusive proof linking saturated fat with heart disease, fat's image was changed for ever.

That's not to say that one could survive solely on a diet of butter, bone marrow, lard, and milkshakes. Too much of anything, from rice cakes to lardy cakes, is never a good thing. The palate would start to tire and the body bloat. A healthy diet means a balanced diet, lots of green stuff, nuts, pulses, fish, and the rest. Fat doesn't kill; rather, too much of the wrong kind can. Allied with sitting on your vast, wobbling butt all day, munching chips by the ton and slurping entire reservoirs of Cherry 7-Up. So in short, embrace animal fats, revel in them, but don't exist solely upon them. And buy the very best you can afford. Fat you can see, wrapped around kidneys or hugging a leg of lamb, is not the stuff to worry about. It's those hidden buggers, creeping around all those processed foods, that are the truly dangerous foe.

'Fat carries flavour and aroma, provides the sexiest of textures, allows us to actually relish in our meat and delight in our food.'

Spaghetti with meatballs

{ SERVES 4 }

1⅛ pounds ground pork

½ pound ground steak or beef

1 whole egg and 1 yolk

¾ cup breadcrumbs, soaked in
½ cup full-fat milk for
10 minutes, then squeezed out

2–5 dried chillies, crumbled

sea salt and freshly ground
black pepper

2 tablespoons olive oil

1 pound dried spaghetti

grated Parmesan, to serve

For the sauce

2 tablespoons olive oil

1½ onions, finely chopped

1-3 fresh Thai or finger chillies,
finely chopped

1 garlic clove, finely chopped

1 (28-ounce) can chopped
tomatoes

8 basil leaves, torn

Italian-American food at its best, star of more mob movies than you can shake a cannoli at. Purists may argue that *Goodfellas*, Martin Scorsese's red-sauce-splashed classic, was the meatball's greatest ever cinematic moment. "Veal, beef, pork . . ." mumbles Vinnie, cooking up his prison feast. "You gotta have the pork. That's the flavour." As well as cutting the garlic with a razor blade. But it's actually in *Point Break*, Kathryn Bigelow's brilliant surf, screw, run, and rob film, where the meatball reaches its peak. So fine is the sandwich that it actually causes the cops, who are on stakeout, to miss the bank being robbed. When done well, meatballs have that sort of effect.

To make the meatballs, mix the pork, beef, egg, egg yolk, breadcrumbs, and chillies together with a good pinch of salt and lots of pepper, then cover and chill for 30 minutes (the mixture, not you).

Meanwhile, to make the sauce, heat the oil in a saucepan, add the onions, chillies, and garlic and cook gently until soft. Add the tomatoes, season, and simmer, uncovered, for 40 minutes. Add the basil at the end of cooking time.

Roll the meat mixture into small, 1½-inch balls. Heat the olive oil over a medium-high heat in a frying pan and fry the meatballs for 2–3 minutes, leaving the inside a little underdone.

Cook the spaghetti in a large saucepan of boiling lightly salted water, following the timing on the pack. Five minutes before the spaghetti is ready, add the meatballs to the sauce and simmer for 5 minutes, until cooked. Drain the pasta and serve with the meatballs, sprinkled with Parmesan.

Chilli cottage pie

{ SERVES 6 }

2 tablespoons olive oil

½–2 Scotch bonnet chillies,
   finely chopped

4 red onions, finely chopped

2¼ pounds ground beef (freshly
   ground if possible)

2 tablespoons tomato purée

4 teaspoons Worcestershire
   sauce, or to taste

Tabasco sauce

2¼ cups fresh beef stock (you
   can use cubes at a push)

sea salt and freshly ground
   black pepper

For the mash

8 large Idaho potatoes, about 3
   pounds total weight, scrubbed

6 tablespoons full-fat milk

4 tablespoons (½ stick) unsalted
   butter, plus 2 tablespoons to
   dot on top

Too often, the cottage pie (and its bleating cousin, the shepherd's pie) is a mean sort of lunch, made with small, rubbery pellets of cheap mince (ground meat), a splash of ketchup, and lumpy mashed potato. Even worse, people insist on using the leftovers from Sunday's roast. I'm all for using up chicken bones and the like, but to chop up yesterday's beef for a pie not only gives an inferior filling—it robs me of roast beef sandwiches, too. My great-grandfather, food writer and polemicist P. Morton Shand, blamed the decline of British food on our culture of leftovers, where ". . . the joint lingered from Sabbath to Sabbath, suffering diverse strange transformations in its progress from Sunday's midday dinner to Saturday's supper: hot, cold; cold, hashed; cold, minced; cold, rissoles; cold, shepherd's pie; cold, Kromensky; and cold, stewed. It is the very diagnosis of dyspepsia." I agree. This recipe uses fresh beef mince. If you can get the decent stuff from your butcher, freshly minced, it does make all the difference. This is a cheap dish, but shouldn't be a mean one. Avoid "lean" mince at all costs.

As to chillies, I like a good kick of warmth, not so much that it sends diners fleeing from the table, their tongues sizzling in bowls of yogurt. I use one or two Scotch bonnets, but adapt as needed. They're pretty fiery, but have a lusciously fruity tang. If you do have to use those generic Holland bell chillies, good luck. They have all the kick of a limbless ass.

For the mash, I don't bother peeling the potatoes before cooking. Boil them in their skins, leave to cool, then peel by hand. Much quicker and easier.

Gently heat the oil in a heavy-bottomed saucepan and soften the chillies in it (do open a window, as these chillies can create a gas that tends to get children crying and wives ticked off), then add the onions and soften for about 10 minutes.

Add the beef, turn the heat to high, and brown it. Add the tomato purée and cook for 2 minutes. Add the Worcestershire sauce, a few dashes of Tabasco, and the stock; taste, then season. Bring to the boil, reduce the heat to low, and simmer for 25 minutes. Preheat the oven to 350°F.

Meanwhile, make the mash. Put the potatoes in a big pan of lightly salted water, bring to the boil, then simmer for 20–25 minutes until a knife goes through with ease. Tip into a colander, let them cool a little, then peel. Heat the milk and butter in a small saucepan until the butter melts, then mash the potatoes with the mixture. Season.

Take a rectangular pie or baking dish and pile in the hot meat. Top with the mash. Fork the top of the mash so it looks like a choppy sea. Dot with a little extra butter and bake for 20–30 minutes, until the top is golden and the meat bubbling fiercely below. Serve with boiled peas.

Beef Stroganoff

{ SERVES 4 }

1⅓ pounds filet steak or
  tenderloin, cut into 2-inch-long
  strips
sea salt and freshly ground
  black pepper
1 teaspoon hot paprika
6 tablespoons (¾ stick) unsalted
  butter
1 tablespoon all-purpose flour
½ cup chicken stock
1 tablespoon tomato purée
1 teaspoon Dijon mustard
4 ounces small mushrooms,
  sliced
1 onion, finely chopped
⅓ cup dry white wine
Scant 1 cup sour cream
2 tablespoons finely chopped
  flat-leaf parsley
boiled long-grain rice and green
  salad, to serve

There are endless arguments as to the origins of beef Stroganoff—whether it was a Hungarian dish, a classic Russian one, or a French one, inspired by Russia. The Stroganovs were a rich and wealthy family of merchants, traders with a long geographical reach. And one of the clan was said to have employed a French chef who is reputed to have created the dish. Other experts disagree, citing the etymology as derived from *strogat*, meaning in Russian to "cut into pieces." The truth is long lost. What remains, though, is a dish that uses sour cream and paprika. Well, sometimes. In other recipes, it uses cream instead. Some marinate the meat, others don't. There is no real "authentic recipe" and this one most certainly isn't. But it's broadly recognizable and tastes damned good, too.

Toss the strips of steak in salt, pepper, and paprika, cover, and put in the fridge for 2 hours.

Melt 2 tablespoons of the butter in a small saucepan over a medium heat, stir in the flour, and cook for 2–3 minutes to make a golden brown roux. Gradually blend in the stock, tomato purée, and mustard, bring to a boil, then simmer for 5–10 minutes until thickened. Set aside.

Heat another 2 tablespoons of the butter in a large frying pan over a medium-high heat and cook the mushrooms for a few minutes. Scoop them out of the pan onto a plate and set aside. Cook the onion in the same pan, adding more butter, if needed, then add to the plate of mushrooms. Cook the steak in the remaining butter until browned on all sides, 3–4 minutes. Deglaze the pan with the wine.

Return the mushrooms and onions to the pan, along with the sauce and sour cream. Mix well, then cover and let stand for 15 minutes. Reheat, sprinkle with chopped parsley, and serve with rice and a green salad.

The perfect burger

There's a lot of guff talked about hamburgers: adding eggs or onions to the mix and topping them with pineapple, sliced beet, foie gras, and God knows what else. I've travelled across America in search of burger perfection and found that one rule applies—the simpler the burger, the better. You still need good meat, minced rump or sirloin with about 20 percent fat, preferably from a butcher. And a small, soft bun that can be held in one hand. Lettuce, tomato, cheese, and bacon are all acceptable, even desirable, additions, not forgetting proper pickles, too. One of the best I've ever eaten was at the In-N-Out burger chain in California. Simple, succulent, and perfect. Byron's is Britain's best chain; for now, anyway. But don't mess about. No monster-size patties or wacky embellishments; just something to be wolfed in about four or five bites, the juices dribbling down your chin.

{ MAKES 8 }

sea salt and freshly ground
  black pepper
2¼ pounds ground beef,
  with at least 20 percent fat
8 slices Cheddar or Swiss cheese
16 rashers smoked
  streaky bacon
8 soft white buns, split
2 beefsteak tomatoes, sliced
1 iceberg lettuce
4 large sweet pickles, halved
mayonnaise, ketchup, and
  mustard, to serve

Add a good pinch of salt to the beef, and lots of pepper. Mix, cover, and leave in the fridge for an hour.

Shape the mixture into 8 patties. Heat a heavy-based pan or barbecue to high, then cook the burgers for about 3 minutes on each side for rare, 4 minutes for medium, and 6 for well done. A minute before they're ready, top them with cheese so it melts slightly.

Fry the bacon until crisp, and toast the buns on the cut sides for 30 seconds.

Now the build. Bottom bun, then burger and cheese, then 2 rashers of bacon, a slice of tomato, a couple of lettuce leaves, and a pickle half. Leave it to personal taste when it comes to the mayo, ketchup, and mustard. Then top bun.

Toad in the hole

¾ cup plus 2 tablespoons all-
 purpose flour
2 medium eggs, beaten
sea salt and freshly ground
 black pepper
¼ cup full-fat milk
3 tablespoons lard or olive oil
1 pound good pork sausages

One of the very few school dishes, along with the ersatz ribs and chips on a Sunday, that I actually found edible. A thrifty lunch, sure, but make sure you get the best sausages you can find (I like chipolatas for this) and it becomes a very decent feast. This is my late stepmother Rose's recipe. She specifies lard, quite rightly, as it adds to the flavour. But olive oil will do fine.

Preheat the oven to 425°F. Sift the flour into a bowl, mix in the eggs, and season. Whisk in the milk to make a smooth batter.

Put 2 tablespoons of the lard or olive oil into a frying pan over a medium heat, then cook the sausages until you have a good colour.

Put the remaining lard or olive oil into a 7 x 11-inch baking or roasting pan and put into the oven for a few minutes, until smoking. Pour one-third of the batter into the pan. When it starts to rise and set in the hot oil, arrange the sausages in it and pour over the rest of the batter. Bake for 25–30 minutes until the batter is browned and billowing.

Roast woodcock

Beguiling brown eyes, an elegant, rapier-like beak, and delicate black markings—the woodcock is an undoubtedly beautiful bird. Agile as a housefly and very hard to shoot. The eating is rather less refined. It arrives at the table roasted whole, neck lolling, and eye staring blindly up. The skull is hewn in half to get at the brains, while the innards lie thick on a piece of fried bread. The flesh is rich, dark, with a hint of the pungent. For those who adore their game, it's the best of the lot.

Any shot bird will have a clean gut (they empty their bowels as they fly), and the entrails are soft and livery in taste. This is based on a recipe from Hugh Fearnley-Whittingstall's magisterial *The River Cottage Meat Book* (Hodder & Stoughton, 2004).

Remove the gizzard: either ask your butcher to do this, or make a small split in the vent end of the bird, insert a finger, and feel for a hard little lump. Spear it with a cocktail stick, pull it out, snip it off, and push the intestines back into the body.

Preheat the oven to 450°F. Put the bird in a roasting pan, massage butter over the breast, and season. Lay the bacon over the breast, then tuck the head and neck under the wing, and put in the hot oven for 8–20 minutes: 8 gives you bloody, 20 well done, I like about 10 minutes. Remove the bacon after 5 minutes, chop, and set aside.

Rest the bird on a warmed plate for 10 minutes. Using a teaspoon, carefully scoop out the innards and set aside. In a small frying pan, heat a little butter and add the bacon. Sizzle for a minute or two, then add the innards and juices from the roasting pan. Add a little red wine, bubble gently for 2 minutes, season, and mash any lumpy bits. Toast the bread, then spread the "pâté" on one half and rest the bird on the other. Gnaw off every last scrap of meat.

{ SERVES 1 }

1 woodcock, plucked but not drawn, head on
a little soft unsalted butter
sea salt and freshly ground black pepper
2 rashers streaky bacon
a little red wine
1 slice of good crusty white bread, halved

Roast grouse

{ SERVES 4 }

4 young grouse

3 tablespoons unsalted butter, softened

sea salt and freshly ground black pepper

⅔ cup dry white wine

1¼ cups game or chicken stock

sprig of thyme

watercress, to serve

For the fried breadcrumbs

7 ounces (4 to 5 slices) white bread, a couple of days old, crusts removed

3 tablespoons unsalted butter

A truly seasonal British treat. I start to get the urge round about the end of July, and by 12th August, when the season starts, I'm craving my first taste. When you have a young bird, it would be heresy to do anything other than roast it, with all the traditional trimmings: clear gravy, fried breadcrumbs, and bread sauce. There's no need for bacon, as it tends to overwhelm the delicate taste.

As to hanging, I don't believe the young birds need it. The Victorians had a taste for birds so "high" that the maggots were already feasting, and the flesh was horribly bitter. Forget all that. The young grouse is a spectacularly unthreatening beast: sweet, succulent, and wonderful. I like mine pink, but not gushing blood. And my father reckons that cold grouse makes the greatest breakfast of all.

Preheat the oven to 475°F. Lightly cover the grouse breasts with butter and season inside and out. Put in a roasting pan and into the searing hot oven for about 15 minutes. You want rare meat, not bloody. The breasts should feel fairly firm. If too soft, they're not cooked. Remove the bird from the pan, and leave to rest while you make the gravy.

Meanwhile, to make the breadcrumbs, tear the bread into small bits and blitz in a food processor to make crumbs. Fry the breadcrumbs in the butter over a medium heat until crisp. Drain on paper towels, then season.

Pour off the excess fat from the roasting pan, then put the pan over a high heat and throw in the wine, stirring and scraping the bottom while you simmer it. Reduce by half, then add the stock, thyme, salt, and pepper and boil to reduce until deeply flavoured. Add any of the juices released from the resting grouse, then strain through a sieve into a warm sauceboat. Serve with watercress, fried breadcrumbs, and bread sauce (see page 28).

Bread sauce

{ MAKES 600 ML/20 FL OZ }

1 onion, halved

6 whole cloves

2½ cups full-fat milk

2 bay leaves

sea salt and freshly ground
   black pepper

7 ounces (4 to 5 slices) white
   bread, a couple of days old,
   crusts removed

½ cup heavy cream

Steaming, and stained dark brown with gravy, bread sauce adds beauty and ballast to whatever it touches. Which is usually chicken or turkey, as any other meats tend to overpower its subtle, clove-scented allure. The key lies in infusing the milk with onion and spices.

Stud the onion with the cloves and put it into a saucepan with the milk, bay leaves, salt, and pepper. Bring to a boil, then take off the heat and leave to stand for 30 minutes.

Tear the bread into small bits and blitz in a food processor to make rough crumbs. Remove the onion and bay leaves from the milk, add the breadcrumbs, and bring gently back to a boil, then simmer over a low heat for about 20 minutes, giving it the occasional stir.

Pour in the cream, bring back to a simmer, and whisk, then serve immediately.

Pot roast chicken

This dish is near impossible to bugger up. The initial browning (to add that extra level of flavour) tends to spit viciously and takes longer than you think. One breast, then the other, then onto its back. Stock cubes are fine, as there's so much else going on, but if you do use them cut back on the salt.

   This is something that's developed over the years. I added the soy and rice wine because they were there and it seemed a good idea at the time. And it worked. The wine gives a rounded, rich sweetness while the soy deepens the flavour of the broth. Don't fear the excess amount of garlic. The cloves soften and mellow in the juices.

Preheat the oven to 350°F. Heat the olive oil in a large cast-iron pan over a medium-high heat and brown the chicken all over, about 10 minutes. Remove the chicken. Shove half the lemon up its ass and squeeze the other half over the skin. Deglaze the pan with the white wine, stirring, then put the chicken back in. Add the garlic, rosemary, stock, rice wine, soy sauce, cilantro stalks, cayenne, salt, and pepper. Bring to a boil.

Cover and roast for 1 hour 10 minutes to 1 hour 20 minutes. To test if the chicken is cooked, poke a skewer into the thickest part of the thigh: the juices should be golden, not pink.

Transfer the chicken to a plate and leave to rest for 10 minutes. In the meantime, strain the cooking liquid through a sieve into another pan; discard the herb stems, but push all the garlic through. Remove excess fat from the top with a spoon, then boil until the liquid is reduced by one-third.

Carve the chicken and place in bowls atop a slice of bread. Pour over your sauce and eat with a crisp, simple romaine lettuce salad. Drink any excess sauce directly from your bowl.

{ SERVES 2–4 }

2 tablespoons olive oil
1 (3–4-pounds) chicken
   (the best you can afford)
1 lemon, halved
⅔ cup dry white wine
10 garlic cloves, unpeeled
2 big sprigs of rosemary
1½ cups chicken stock (fresh or
   cube)
¼ cup Shaoxing rice wine
2 tablespoons soy sauce
handful of cilantro stalks
2 pinches of cayenne pepper
   (optional, but gives it a
   wonderful heat)
sea salt and freshly ground
   black pepper
thick slices of brown bread,
   to serve
romaine lettuce salad, to serve

A deeply healthy, utterly addictive noodle dish

{ SERVES 2 }

2 chicken breasts (the best you
   can afford), cut into ½-inch
   cubes
juice of 1 lime
2 teaspoons *gochujang* (Korean
   chilli paste) or a good whack
   of fish sauce
2 tiny chopped bird's-eye chillies
a splash of soy sauce

For the stir-fry
9 ounces Thai rice noodles
dash of peanut oil
3 garlic cloves, finely chopped
4 scallions, sliced into
   1-inch pieces diagonally
½ head of broccoli (about 5
   ounces), cut into small florets
8 Thai or banana shallots,
   finely sliced
8 baby corn, quartered
⅓ cup frozen peas
¼–½ cup chicken stock (a cube
   is fine)
3–10 bird's-eye chillies, finely
   chopped (depending how hot
   you like it)
2 teaspoons fish sauce
big handful of cilantro
   leaves, roughly chopped
small handful of mint leaves,
   roughly chopped
1 lime, halved

This is probably the dish I cook more than any other, and we eat it at least twice a week at home. There was much debate as to whether it belonged in the "From far-flung shores" chapter, but in the end I decided this was comfort, pure and simple. Eating it makes me feel happy, wholesome even.

You can use whatever vegetables you have to hand, from frozen peas to broccoli, sugar snaps, French beans, or bean sprouts. It even makes that ridiculous baby corn look useful. The key is a balance between the hot, sour, and salty. The flavours are bold, but never overwhelming.

It's the sort of food that renders talking irrelevant. Just writing about these noodles makes my mouth water. My wife describes them as "medicinal," thanks to all the fresh vegetables, herbs, and chillies within. We like it hot, but tone down the chillies if need be. And you can always add more heat, by way of the chillies in the fish sauce. If you can't get hold of those fiendish little scud or bird's eye chillies, use a quarter of the amount of habanero or Scotch bonnet. The flavour is different, but the heat mighty.

There are two slightly exotic ingredients here, both easily available on the Internet or from Asian shops. They make the dish better still, but are not essential. The first is *gochujang*, a Korean fermented chilli paste that I use in the marinade. It has a deep, rich flavour with a hint of Marmite. And the second are the noodles I use (Khanom Jeen Rice Noodles 200g), specialist noodles used by the Thais for breakfast and curries. They have a wonderful soft texture. If you can't get them, use any rice noodles. I have a pair of special white bowls we use for this soup, deep and wide. They are as much a part of the ritual as are the noodles themselves.

{ CONTINUES OVERLEAF }

For the chilli fish sauce

⅓ cup fish sauce

4–8 bird's-eye chillies,
   finely chopped

juice of 1 lime

This is best cooked in a wok, and the chicken must be cut into small cubes of roughly the same size, to ensure they cook evenly. Make it in two batches. The actual cooking takes a few minutes. Once the prep is done, you're laughing.

Put the chicken in a bowl with the lime juice and *gochujang*. Cover and leave to marinate in the fridge for an hour. Remove from the fridge 10 minutes before cooking.

To make the chilli fish sauce, mix all the ingredients together and set aside.

For the stir-fry, cook the rice noodles in a large pan of boiling water according to the package instructions. Drain, cool under cold running water, and set aside.

Drain the chicken, discard the marinade, and pat the chicken dry with paper towels.

Heat the peanut oil in a wok until smoking, then throw in half the garlic, cook for a second, then add half the chicken and stir until browned, 1–2 minutes.

Add half of all the vegetables, but not the chillies. Stir-fry for another 30 seconds, then add half the stock and chillies. Taste, season with fish sauce, and cook for 30 seconds to a minute more until the chicken is cooked through. Add half the herbs, mix, and add half the noodles. Mix for another 30 seconds and finish with the juice of half a lime.

Repeat for the second bowl. Serve with chilli fish sauce.

Chicken & sweet corn soup

This is the sort of soup best suited to the lean, cruel months of January and February. So it's a bore that the very best sweet corn is out of season. Still, use the imported stuff if it has sufficient sweetness. Or freeze a glut in the summer and autumn months. This is not the place for a stock cube: using my 5-hour stock (see page 39) will produce something that is rich, soothing, and restorative.

Bring the stock to the boil in a large saucepan and simmer, uncovered, for 15 minutes to reduce a little.

Add the corn kernels to the stock and cook for 2 minutes. Stir in the shredded chicken and simmer for 5 minutes more until cooked through. Add the scallions and lemon juice and season to taste with salt, pepper, and a dash of Tabasco. Serve.

{ **SERVES 4** }

5 cups dark chicken stock (see page 39)

2 ears of corn, kernels cut from the cobs

½ pound boneless cooked chicken (the best you can afford), shredded

2 scallions, sliced

juice of ½ lemon

sea salt and freshly ground black pepper

Tabasco sauce

My mother's roast chicken

{ SERVES 4 }

1 unwaxed lemon
1 (4-pound) chicken (the
  best you can afford), rinsed
  inside and out with cold
  water and then drained
sea salt and freshly ground
  black pepper
about 6 tablespoons (¾ stick)
  unsalted butter, at room
  temperature

Gravy
Scant 1 cup dry white wine
Scant 2 cups chicken stock
  (a cube is fine)

My wife swore that if she heard me mention this dish one more time, she'd shove it where the sun don't beam. Well, words to that effect. Because this was such a staple of my youth, I roll it out any time anyone asks if my mother is a good cook—which is pretty much all of the time. She is, although she was always less bothered with the cakes, puddings, and pies side of things: anything that requires exact measurements. Which was fine by us. All my sister and I really wanted was Findus Crispy Pancakes and Ice Magic chocolate sauce. Sadly, we had to seek those illicit pleasures elsewhere.

This is a classic recipe, cooked in the top right-hand oven of the Aga. I've adapted it for normal ovens. My mother insists that chopping off that dangly bit above the cavity and putting it on top of the bird improves the flavour. As it releases about a ton of schmaltz, or chicken fat, I'd agree. Buy the best chicken you can afford. Rather eat one decent free-range than four of those flabby imported beasts with all the depth of a puddle.

Preheat the oven to 425°F. Pierce the lemon with a small knife and "shove it up the chicken's bottom." Season the bird with salt and pepper, inside and out, then massage the butter all over it. Place in a roasting pan. Cook for 20 minutes, then turn the oven down to 350°F and cook for 40 minutes more. Poke a skewer into the thickest part of the thigh: the juices should be golden, not pink. If not, cook for a little longer, then retest. Let it rest for 15–20 minutes.

Meanwhile, for the gravy, spoon excess fat from the roasting pan, but leave a little in the pan. Put the pan over a high heat. When everything starts bubbling, deglaze with the white wine. Simmer while the alcohol cooks off, then add the stock, stirring all the time. Tip in any juices from the resting chicken. Boil to reduce a little, then strain through a sieve into a warm sauceboat. Serve the chicken with the gravy.

Chicken & mushroom pie

Nothing beats a good pie when nights are long and credit short. I'm far too lazy to make my own puff pastry, especially when the supermarkets have decent ready-made stuff. Just ensure it's all-butter, as the pastry made with margarine is predictably nasty. When roasting a chicken for dinner, add another one to eat later. As ever, the better the chicken, the finer the taste and texture.

Melt 3 tablespoons of the butter in a saucepan over a low heat, then stir in the flour (one of those small Wonder Whisks makes life much easier) and cook for about 2 minutes. Don't let it colour. Slowly add the hot stock until you have a thick sauce. Season, then add the mustard, lemon juice, and a few dashes of Tabasco and leave to simmer for 2 minutes.

Sauté the onion and the fresh and soaked mushrooms in the remaining butter until soft. Add the wine, bring to a boil to cook off the alcohol, then add the mixture to the sauce, stirring over a medium heat for a couple of minutes. Add the chicken and herbs, then allow to cool.

Preheat the oven to 400°F. Put the chicken mixture into a 2-quart pie or baking dish and brush the edge with a little beaten egg. Roll out the pastry on a lightly floured surface and lift onto the pie dish. Cut a couple of small vents in the pastry and press around the edges to seal well. Brush with beaten egg and bake for 30–35 minutes, or until golden brown.

{ SERVES 4–6 }

6 tablespoons (¾ stick) unsalted butter

⅓ cup all-purpose flour, sifted, plus extra for rolling pastry

2½ cups hot chicken stock

sea salt and freshly ground black pepper

2 teaspoons Dijon mustard

juice of 1 lemon

Tabasco sauce

1 large onion, finely chopped

8 ounces fresh button mushrooms, sliced

½ ounce dried morel mushrooms, soaked in warm water, drained, and chopped (optional, as they are expensive, but they do add some mycological magic)

⅔ cup dry white wine

1 cold roasted chicken (the best you can afford), flesh stripped and cut into bite-size pieces

1 tablespoon finely chopped tarragon

1 tablespoon finely chopped flat-leaf parsley

1 egg, beaten, to glaze

1½ pound all-butter puff pastry

{ Chicken stock }

Stock used to scare the hell out of me. Not literally. It never chased me through the woods with a bloody cleaver, or harangued me on the Second Coming of Christ. No, my fear of stock was purely practical. Unlike frying an egg, say, or making a curry, it seemed to involve vast, industrial vats overflowing with centuries of serious culinary know-how. I saw it as a professional process, mastered by moustachioed French chefs, their hands riddled with scars, their toques white and priapic. "The foundation of French cuisine," they'd mutter, in gutteral Gallic, before browning a few kilos of chicken wings in a world-weary way.

But one day, fed up with the impotent insipidity of the store-bought versions, I gave it a go. I followed a recipe, probably by Nigel Slater, and managed to transform a couple of old carcasses, along with a few tired vegetables squatting in the bottom of my fridge, into a golden nectar, good enough to drink. I had created something wonderful from the drab, useless, and everyday. Bless you, kitchen chemistry. You never cease to amaze. And so I became a maker of stock, a process every bit as soothing as it is satisfactory.

As the years have passed, so my stock recipe has evolved. Dark chicken stock is my liquid of choice, made from at least two carcasses (frozen leftovers from a roast chicken—when there are two foil-wrapped parcels in the deep freeze, it's time to make stock) and roasted wings. These wings, I reckon, are the secret weapons, although necks and hearts are grand, too. No liver though, as it adds an unpleasant bitter note. Very occasionally, towards the end of the winter, I might throw in a grouse that has lurked in the icy depths too long. Or a partridge carcass. The more flavour, the better, especially as the vast majority of my stock goes into either spicy, Thai-tinged broths or proper risottos that crave a serious savoury punch.

Although it can be a good way of using up carrots sulking in the depths of one's fridge, the fresher the vegetables, the better the stock will taste. Contrary to traditional knowledge, stock is *not* a rubbish dump for geriatric onions and rotten tomatoes, nor should it be left forever bubbling, as you throw in whatever seems fit. Tomatoes add sweetness, as do onions (keep their skin on for colour). Celery adds . . . well, celery is the most mysterious of vegetables. Raw, it's pretty dull and one-noted. Cooked down, it adds a sensual roundness that a stock cannot live without. A few parsley and cilantro stalks add still more depth (I just freeze them after using the leaves), along with peppercorns and a brace of bay leaves.

Every cook will have his or her own version. Purists will go for bones alone, Michelin-starred maestros might favour a very light stock, cooked for no more than an hour or two, so as not to overwhelm. But I'm an eater, not a saucier, and I want a lot of roasted chicken heft. So mine takes about 5 hours. At the meekest of simmers. I plunge my roasted carcasses and wings into cold water (and a big stockpot is a must; up there with a good knife and proper wok, it's a stalwart of my kitchen), bring to a boil, skim off the scum, then turn down the heat until it's just a flickering flame, add the vegetables, herbs, and aromatics, and let it blip away. Just a blip, mind, not even a simmer. When the cooking time is up, taste, sieve, and pour into pitchers or large measuring cups to cool. Let the dark sediment settle at the bottom, then pour off the clear liquid and use or freeze. It's ready for risotto.

For broth, I reduce it by about a third to intensify the flavour. To clarify further, there are endless clever ways with egg whites and mince. But I'm buggered if I know what they are. My stock is for cooking, slurping, and sipping, so I don't lose too much sleep over a few minuscule and flavour-packed specks. This is cooking as therapy, a balm and salve. And you get a few quarts of amber nectar at the end. Super stock, indeed.

A darkish, deeply flavoured chicken stock

{ MAKES ABOUT 5 LITRES / 9 PINTS }

2 cooked chicken carcasses, kept from roast chicken
8 chicken wings, roasted for 20 minutes at 450°F
chicken neck and heart (optional but preferable)
2 large tomatoes, quartered
2 large onions, quartered
2 large carrots, roughly chopped
3 celery stalks, roughly chopped (with leaves, if present)
handful of mixed parsley and cilantro stalks
2 bay leaves
8 black peppercorns

Cut or tear up the carcasses into small pieces and put into a large stockpot, along with the wings and neck and heart, if using. Cover with cold water (filtered is best; it sounds poncey, but it does make a difference to the flavour) and bring to a boil. Skim off any scum and turn down the heat.

Add the tomatoes, vegetables, herbs, and peppercorns and cook for 5 hours, covered, over a flickering flame. You want blip blip, not bubble bubble.

Use a slotted spoon to discard all the meat and vegetables. Pour the liquid through a fine sieve into pitchers or large measuring cups. Leave it to sit and cool.

After an hour, most of the sediment will drop to the bottom of the pitchers. Skim off excess fat—but leave some. Pour the stock into freezer bags, leaving the sediment behind.

A really good fish pie

2½ cups full-fat milk

½ small onion, thinly sliced

6 whole black peppercorns

1 bay leaf

2 fresh parsley stalks

blade of mace

⅔ pound undyed smoked
    haddock

¼ pound cod fillets

⅔ cup dry white wine

Tabasco sauce

½ pound small cooked prawns,
    shelled

1 small pot (about 2 ounces)
    potted shrimps (see page 49)

24 uncooked scallops, about
    ½ pound (optional)

big pinch of finely chopped
    flat-leaf parsley

For the mash

3 pounds Idaho potatoes,
    scrubbed

sea salt and freshly ground black
    pepper

6 tablespoons full-fat milk

4 tablespoons (½ stick) unsalted
    butter, plus 2 tablespoons to
    dot on top

There's no place for salmon in a proper fish pie. I'm sorry, but it's just not right. It's somehow too greasy, too lurid, and too, well, salmony, to feel anything but ill at ease. It's not that I hate salmon. The wild stuff is a rare treat, rich and magnificent. And there are a couple of decent salmon farmers (Loch Duart, for one) that allow these once-great beasts space to swim and build up their muscles and fins. But the vast majority of farmed stuff is pap, pure and simple. Ruinous to the environment, and equally dull on the palate. Smoked haddock, on the other hand, is the backbone of this pie. Undyed, of course, alongside some good unsmoked fish, for contrast and balance. A few prawns add life, and queen scallops are a fine addition, too. Even a pot or two of potted shrimps. A good béchamel is essential, and a whisper of booze. But eggs are just gilding the lily. This pie is all about the fish.

To make the mash, put the potatoes in a big pan of salted water, bring to the boil, then simmer for 20–25 minutes until a knife goes through with ease. Tip into a colander, let them cool down a little, then peel. Heat the milk and butter in a small saucepan until the butter melts, then mash the potatoes with the milk. Season.

Preheat the oven to 350°F. Put the milk, onion, peppercorns, bay leaf, parsley stalks, and mace in a large shallow pan, heat to a simmer. Then add the smoked haddock and cod

{ CONTINUES OVERLEAF }

For the béchamel sauce

4 tablespoons (½ stick) unsalted
  butter

⅓ cup all-purpose flour

2 tablespoons heavy cream

white pepper

and poach for 5–6 minutes until the fish just flakes when pressed with a knife. Lift out the fish, remove the skin and any stray bones, and set aside. Strain the milk through a sieve into a measuring cup; discard the flavourings. If necessary, add a little extra milk to make 2½ cups; set aside.

To make the béchamel sauce, melt the butter in a saucepan over a low heat, stir in the flour using a wooden spoon, and cook for 2–3 minutes; do not let it brown. Remove from the heat and slowly stir in the reserved milk until smooth. Add the cream and cook for 2–3 minutes, adding salt and white pepper to taste.

Add the wine to the béchamel and cook gently, stirring, for 2–3 minutes more. Add a big dash of Tabasco. Add the fish, shellfish, and chopped parsley and put into a pie dish.

Cover the fish mixture with the mash; using a fork, fluff up the top into small waves and dot with a little extra butter. Put in the oven for 20–30 minutes, until the top is golden.

Haddock Parker Bowles

2 plum tomatoes

4 tablespoons (½ stick)
  unsalted butter

4 (6-ounce) undyed smoked
  haddock fillets, skinned

4 eggs

For the white wine sauce

2 large shallots, finely chopped

2 tablespoons unsalted butter

¾ cup dry white wine

⅔ cup fish stock

⅔ cup heavy cream

juice of ½ lemon

For the mash

1½ pounds Idaho potatoes,
  scrubbed

3 tablespoons full-fat milk

2 tablespoons (¼ stick) unsalted
  butter

sea salt and freshly ground
  black pepper

1 ounce chives, chopped

My grandfather was a good cook, in a time when gentlemen were rarely seen in the kitchen. My father has a picture of him in his apron, looking very pukka. It was probably made on Savile Row. My uncle Simon carried on the family tradition with Green's, a proper English restaurant and oyster bar. It has the feeling of a St. James's club, although the food is markedly superior. And Haddock Parker Bowles could be described as a signature dish. It's certainly never been off the menu since the first restaurant opened in St. James's in 1982 (there's now another Green's in Cornhill, in the City). The current recipe is wonderful, but a little too cheffy for my tastes (in the cooking, not the eating). So I've pared it down a little, although the essence remains. Make the tomato *concassé* first, along with the sauce, which can be reheated. And poach the eggs just after you've made the mash.

First, make the tomato *concassé*. Pierce the tomatoes, then put them in a bowl of boiling water for 30 seconds. Run them under the cold tap. Peel, cut into quarters, remove the seeds, and cut the flesh into small dice.

To make the sauce, sweat the shallots in the butter over a medium–low heat until soft and just turning golden. Combine the white wine and stock and use to deglaze the pan, then reduce slowly until lightly syrupy. Add the cream and reduce until the sauce coats the back of a spoon.

{ CONTINUES OVERLEAF }

Strain through a sieve, then add the lemon juice. Season and keep warm.

Make the mash. Put the potatoes in a big pan of salted water, bring to a boil, then simmer for 20–25 minutes until a knife goes through with ease. Tip them into a colander, let them cool a little, then peel. Heat the milk and butter in a saucepan until the butter melts, then mash the potatoes with the milk. Season, mix with the chives, and keep warm.

For the fish, melt the butter in a large frying pan over a medium heat and fry the haddock fillets for about 8 minutes until brown and the fish flakes easily when pressed with a knife, turning halfway through cooking. Allow to rest.

Poach the eggs (see my method on page 51), then drain.

To serve, put the chive mash on 4 warmed plates, top with haddock and a poached egg. Pour the sauce around the fish, and sprinkle with the tomato *concassé*.

Goujons of sole, haddock, or even pollack (if you must)

{ SERVES 4 }

10½ ounces white bread,
  a couple of days old, no crusts
1½ cups all-purpose flour
sea salt and freshly ground
  black pepper
4 eggs, beaten
2 pounds 4 ounces sole, cod,
  haddock, plaice, or pollack,
  filleted, skinned, and cut into
  strips somewhere between the
  size of your small and ring
  fingers
6 tablespoons olive oil
3 lemons, cut into wedges

For the pea purée
2 pounds frozen petits pois
2 tablespoons (¼ stick) salted
  butter
a few sprigs of mint
splash of hot chicken stock

A *goujon* is a fish finger with a French accent and Chanel bag. They're incredibly easy to make and it's a lunch that the children love as much as we do. Sole is expensive, but perfect. If buying haddock, make sure it's sustainably caught—the same with cod and plaice. Rather than have me wagging my finger at you, check out the Monterey Bay Aquarium website to see which fish you can and can't eat (www.montereybayaquarium.org). Some people suggest pollack. But there's a reason we haven't eaten this fish for years . . . it's deadly dull. As my friend Matthew Fort would say, "Bollocks to pollacks."

Tear the bread into small pieces and blitz in a food processor to make crumbs, then put them on a plate. Mix the flour with a little salt and pepper and lay out on another plate. Put the eggs in a shallow dish.

Using one hand (this stops both hands getting clagged up), dip the fish strips into the flour, then the egg, then the breadcrumbs, shaking off any excess at each stage.

Fry the fish in batches in a couple of tablespoons of olive oil over a medium–high heat, until crisp and golden, then drain on paper towels. Keep hot while cooking the rest.

For the pea purée, cook the peas in a saucepan of boiling water for 4–5 minutes, then drain. Put them into a blender, add the butter and mint, and blend, adding hot chicken stock to thin it out as needed; I like it to be quite thick, so you can use the *goujons* as golden spoons. Season and serve with the *goujons* and wedges of lemon.

Baked potatoes with caviar

{ **SERVES 4** }

4 small floury baking potatoes,
  such as Idaho
2 tablespoons sour cream
4 tablespoons (½ stick)
  unsalted butter
4 ounces caviar

OK, so this is a rare treat. And with wild sturgeon in perilous decline, a ruinously expensive one, too. But there is some first-class farmed caviar out there, miles removed from that muddy muck from years gone by. I once went to a caviar tasting with Laura King, the real expert on all matters ovoid and salted. With me was chef Rowley Leigh and food writer Bill Knott. She opened a vast 5 kg/11 lb tin of wild beluga (the biggest of the caviar eggs, the rarest and most expensive, though in my view no better or worse than oscietra, just different). We all took polite nibbles, but for Bill, the temptation was too much. When Laura turned her back, he dug deep and emerged with a mass of these oily black eggs piled atop his mother-of-pearl spoon. A huge gash now marked the previously pristine surface, christened by Laura as "the Knott Trench."

As a deeply greedy person, and a caviar freak, I'd rather eat a glut or nothing at all. The contrast of cool eggs and hot, creamy potato is one of the best in the world. It'll probably cost you the same as dinner for two at Le Gavroche. In its own way, and eaten rarely, it's every bit as good.

Preheat the oven to 425°F. Bake the potatoes for about 45 minutes until crisp and soft inside.

Carefully cut open the potatoes and scoop the insides into a bowl. Add the sour cream and butter, mix until the butter melts, then spoon back into the potatoes.

Heap with caviar and eat at once.

Potted shrimps

There are many claimants to the crustacean throne, with various lobsters and crabs elbowing their way into our affections. But the modest brown shrimp, *Crangon crangon*, is a definite contender. The only prawn we call a shrimp (unlike the Americans, who call all prawns shrimp), it's small and intensely sweet. The best in the world come from Morecambe Bay in Lancashire. Potting is one of those old British techniques that has fallen by the wayside, but before the invention of refrigeration, covering cooked beef, ham, crab, or lobster with a layer of butter didn't just add to the flavour, it preserved, too. Serve cold with slices of brown bread and butter, or hot on good toast.

{ SERVES 6 }

12 tablespoons (1½ sticks) unsalted butter
1 teaspoon ground black pepper
½ teaspoon ground cayenne pepper
½ teaspoon ground mace
1 small bay leaf
1 pound peeled brown shrimps
sea salt
brown bread, sliced, to serve
3 lemons, cut into wedges, to serve

In a saucepan over a medium–low heat, melt the butter, then add the black pepper, cayenne, mace, and bay leaf. Throw in the shrimps and stir to coat. Cook for a couple of minutes until brown and cooked, then remove from the heat and set aside until just warm. Remove the bay leaf and check the seasoning.

Divide the shrimp mixture among 6 ramekins and season with a little salt. The butter should cover the shrimps. Put the mixture into the fridge and chill until set.

Toast the brown bread; serve with the potted shrimps and a wedge of lemon.

{ Eggs }

I once spent an entire week going to work on a diet of eggs. Eggs and pretty much nothing else. I was allowed butter or oil to cook them in, as well as herbs, chillies, onions, and any other secondary ingredient deemed appropriate to the matter in hand. A little cheese or ham could creep in for an omelette, say, but mustn't become the star of the show. Bacon was a no-no, despite my protestations (fried eggs cry out for crisp shavings of smoked, cured pork), and mayonnaise *verboten*. This ovoid diet wasn't done for pleasure, I hasten to add, nor culinary curiosity. Nope, it was a commissioned piece for the *Mail on Sunday* in reaction to news of the Charles Saatchi diet. The great advertising guru and contemporary art collector had lost huge amounts of weight on a similar diet, despite being married to Nigella Lawson. A triumph of the will, if I ever heard one. And I was to sample a mere seven days.

The first day was fine. Boiled egg for breakfast, fried egg sandwich for lunch, masala scrambled eggs for dinner. The next day started with a poached pair on toast, and a craving for anything, anything but egg. I walked past sausage shops and curry houses, burger joints and brasseries, longing for a change. Lunch was another omelette, eaten resentfully. And by dinner, my baked egg became a figure of hate. Five more long, dreary, and frustrating days followed. My digestion shut up shop, my burps became toxic . . . I became toxic. Damn you, eggs. Once the experiment was over, I didn't touch another for at least a month.

Despite the occasional blip, though, I love eggs, worship their curves, adore them in their every form. Fried in butter and plonked between two slices of cheap white bread or whisked into still more butter to make hollandaise sauce. Boiled with soldiers, baked with ham, coddled, scrambled, and poached. Even raw, draped over steak tartare. They're the ultimate convenience food, perfectly packaged and endlessly versatile. French cuisine would be lost without them. Actually, most of mankind would have problems making do without them.

Eggs cover every base, from economy food (tortilla, say) to comfort (baked eggs), home cooking (scrambled eggs) to haute cuisine (*oeufs à la neige*). Hen eggs might be our staple, but duck and goose eggs have a special richness all of their own. Don't even get me started on eggs from fish.

But too often we forget the basics. There was uproar when Delia Smith started her *How to Cook* with boiling an egg. "Outrage!" cried the snobs. "Off with her head!" bellowed the buffoons. Surely, they moaned, everyone knew how to boil an egg? Well, they don't. It's not difficult, but there are a few factors to take into account. How fresh is the egg (particularly important when it comes to poached eggs), how big, and exactly how hard do you like your white? I have no problem with it being a little "spermy," but my wife cannot bear the sight of uncooked albumen. So while not attempting to teach my grandmother to, *ahem*, suck eggs, these recipes all work for me.

There is much debate about how to poach eggs. You need a shallow saucepan with a lid. Bring salted water to a boil in the pan. Break the eggs into ramekins (the fresher the eggs, the better). Turn off the heat, then drop in the eggs. Leave them for 3 minutes, then lift out with a slotted spoon and blot with paper towels.

As with chicken and pigs, I do believe free-range eggs are superior to those produced by barn-reared chickens; if it doesn't say "organic" or "free-range," assume the worst. The difference in taste is huge. Dull, insipid, and watery, eggs from barn-reared chickens are the end product of a wretched life. And they are a waste of money, too. Rather eat one decent egg than two second-rate ones.

Fresh eggs are best and, if you're lucky enough to have chickens, then yee-ha: you can date the eggs with easy precision. In fact, the eggs from my father's chickens are the best I've ever tasted. His birds eat better than we do, with veggie scraps and grit to keep the shells hard. But buy the freshest you can find (difficult in a supermarket). A good test is to drop an egg in a glass of water (not convenient for the aisles of Asda or Sainsbury's, I know). If it drops to the bottom, it's fresh. The further it floats towards the surface, the older it is. If it bobs gaily on the top, bin it.

Chorizo scrambled eggs

{ SERVES 4 }

olive oil, for frying

7 ounces soft picante chorizo,
  sliced into ½-inch-thick pieces

¼ cup stale white bread, diced

8 eggs, beaten

sea salt and freshly
  ground pepper

½ teaspoon dried red chilli
  flakes

2 tablespoons flat-leaf parsley,
  roughly chopped

fried potatoes, to serve
  (optional)

This is all about texture and contrast. Frazzled chorizo, crisp bread, and wobbling, just-set egg. A Spanish classic.

Heat a dash of olive oil in a frying pan and fry the chorizo over a medium–high heat until it begins to crisp. Add the diced bread and fry, stirring from time to time, until brown.

Stir in the eggs, season, and add the chilli. Turn the heat down to extremely low and scramble the eggs very slowly for 15–20 minutes, stirring all the time, until soft and creamy. Sprinkle with chopped parsley and serve with fried potatoes, if you wish.

Baked eggs

{ SERVES 2 }

a little chopped ham or cooked
  asparagus (optional)
4 eggs
2–3 tablespoons heavy cream
4 teaspoons unsalted butter
sea salt and freshly ground
  black pepper
hot toast, to serve

This is one of my mother's "signature" dishes, although
she'd be perplexed as to what a "signature" dish is. When
we used to arrive home, late, from holiday, the house would
be cold and dark, the fridge bare. But my sister and I would
collect the eggs, and my mother would break them into
ramekins, splosh in a little cream from the top of the milk
bottle, and dot with butter.

Preheat the oven to 350°F.

If using ham or asparagus, divide this between 2 ramekins.
Break the eggs into the ramekins, then add the cream,
butter, salt, and pepper.

Put into a small roasting pan and pour in some just-boiled
water to come halfway up the sides of the ramekins. Bake
for 7–10 minutes until the yolk is wobbling and the white
just set. Serve with toast.

Fried eggs

{ SERVES 1 }

Ah, the great dilemma—butter or goose fat? The latter is better for a serious treat, but the former should be the default option. Olive oil is fine, but it does seem a wasted opportunity. Butter and egg are the closest of friends.

1 egg
2 tablespoons (¼ stick) salted
  butter
sea salt and freshly ground
  black pepper

Break the egg into a ramekin. Heat a small frying pan over medium heat, add the butter, and heat until it is just bubbling. Slip in the egg.

Tidy up any edges—the older the egg is, the more the white will sprawl across the pan—and keep basting the egg using a spoon. Pay close attention to the yolk, but don't overbaste.

Once the yolk takes on an opaque sheen, the white is set, and the edges a touch frilly (up to 3 minutes, depending on size), remove with a spatula and blot with a piece of paper towel. Season and serve.

Tortilla

{ SERVES 4 }

4 tablespoons olive oil

2 onions, ideally Spanish yellow,
  thinly sliced

2 waxy potatoes, peeled and cut
  into small dice

pinch of crushed chillies

8 eggs, beaten

sea salt and freshly ground
  black pepper

There are two important factors to the perfect tortilla. First, the right-size pan is crucial. You need a small frying pan, about 6 inches in diameter. As these Spanish potato and onion omelettes are perfect for everything from breakfast to picnics, it's well worth the investment. The second lies in the caramelization of the onions. . . low and slow, so that golden hue is teased out, adding immeasurable depth to the flavour. You want a gently oozing center, too.

Heat half the oil in a large frying pan, add the onions, and cook over a low heat for at least 30 minutes until soft and golden. Add the potatoes and chillies, increase the heat a little, and cook for another 20 minutes until the potatoes are golden with a hint of crust. Tip everything into a bowl and leave to cool slightly.

When cool, add the beaten eggs, season, and mix. Heat the remaining olive oil in a 6-inch frying pan until hot, then add the egg and potato mixture and cook for 4 minutes, using a spatula to run around the edge.

When the bottom of the omelette is firm, flip it out of the pan onto a plate, put the pan back on the heat, and slip in the omelette, uncooked side down. Cook for 3–4 minutes more, until nearly set, then turn out and cut into 4 pieces.

Huevos rancheros

You'll find this classic breakfast dish all over Mexico and the southwestern United States, and it ranks up alongside bacon and eggs as the royalty of the breakfast boys. It's the perfect early morning heart-starter, the sauce possessing just enough kick to jolt the senses into action, while that yolk softens everything. You can cook the sauce in advance, to make things easier. And do try to get proper corn tortillas, as that maize tang is truly the soul of Mexican food. You can use those El Paso versions from the supermarket—but they just don't taste the same.

{ SERVES 2 }

1 pound tomatoes
peanut oil, for frying
1–3 fresh jalapeño peppers,
  finely chopped
sea salt and freshly ground
  black pepper
pinch of superfine sugar
2 small corn tortillas
2 eggs

Pierce the tomatoes, then put them in a bowl of boiling water for 30 seconds. Run them under the cold tap. Peel, cut into quarters, remove and discard the seeds, and then finely chop the flesh.

Heat 1–2 tablespoons oil in a heavy-based frying pan, add the tomatoes and jalapeños, and cook over a low heat for about 25 minutes, or until the tomatoes are reduced to a thick sauce. Season to taste with salt, pepper, and a pinch of sugar.

In another frying pan, heat a little oil and fry the tortillas for a few seconds on each side, to soften. Drain on paper towels, wrap in foil, and keep warm.

Fry the eggs in the same pan, adding more oil if needed, until the whites are set but the yolks are still runny.

To serve, put a warm tortilla on each plate, top with a fried egg, and then spoon on some tomato sauce, leaving the yolk exposed.

"Gegs (9–4)"*

{ SERVES 2 }

* **Scrambled eggs**

6 eggs
sea salt and freshly ground
    black pepper
4 tablespoons (½ stick) salted
    butter
hot toast, to serve

This is a beautiful cryptic-crossword clue. Slow and low is the key. You want fat, creamy curds, rather than rubbery globules of overcooked protein. The only way to guarantee this is to cook them over the lowest possible heat. Use a heat diffuser if you have one. If not, use the lowest flame and remove the pan from the heat if it gets too hot. There's no need for milk or cream; just good, fresh eggs, butter, salt, and pepper.

Break the eggs into a bowl, add 1 teaspoon of water, a pinch of salt, and a twist of pepper, and mix with a fork. Don't beat the hell out of them, just do enough for them to get to know each other better.

Heat the butter in a saucepan until it just about melts. Pour in the eggs and stir over the lowest possible heat. You don't want anything to happen for at least 5–7 minutes. Keep stirring, stretching those curds. Slowly, very slowly, the eggs will start to firm up. If it happens too quickly, remove the pan from the heat. After 15–20 minutes, they will be ready. Serve on hot toast.

Variation
Finely chop a small onion and a red chilli, then sizzle in half the butter until soft; allow to cool slightly. Add the remaining butter and melt, then add the eggs mixed with 1 teaspoon water and seasoning and cook as above. Two minutes before they are ready, add 1 peeled, seeded, and finely chopped tomato and a handful of finely chopped fresh cilantro.

Mayonnaise

Everyone used to tell me how easy mayonnaise was to make. I'd try it, split the bugger and give up for another few years. But then came the breakthrough. Some patient chef explained that, aside from making sure the eggs are at room temperature, it's all about the initial emulsion of oil and yolk. Keep the faith and add the oil, a drop at a time, until you have that thick base. After that you can add the oil in a thin stream. The rest is easy. Use a bowl with a narrow base and perch it on a tea towel to prevent slipping.

Put the yolks, mustard, salt, and pepper in a bowl and whisk together for a good minute. The mustard helps the emulsion and the salt helps thicken.

Add a tiny drop of the sunflower oil and whisk hard. Once amalgamated, add a drop more and repeat. Keep doing this until the mixture starts to thicken, then you can get a bit more free with the pouring. But keep whisking and make sure the mixture emulsifies before you add more oil. Add the rest of the sunflower oil in a steady stream, whisking all the time, then slowly pour in the olive oil and continue to whisk. Once all the oil is used, taste and adjust the seasoning, add the lemon juice, and whisk again. If it's too thick, whisk in a couple of teaspoons of warm water.

{ MAKES ABOUT 1¼ CUPS }

2 egg yolks, at room temperature
1 teaspoon Dijon mustard
sea salt and freshly ground
  black pepper
1 cup sunflower oil
⅓ cup extra-virgin olive oil
big squeeze of lemon juice

French onion soup

{ SERVES 8–10 }

½ pound plus 5 tablespoons
(2 sticks plus 5 tablespoons)
unsalted butter
8 large Spanish onions, sliced
as thin as possible (a
mandoline is perfect for this)
salt and freshly ground
black pepper
1½ teaspoons all-purpose flour
⅔ cup dry white wine (or a glug
of Port if you want a slightly
sweeter, richer note)
¼ cup sherry vinegar or
red wine vinegar
a few sprigs of thyme
2 quarts hot beef or dark brown
chicken stock (see page 39)
1 baguette, cut into thin slices
2–3 tablespoons olive oil
6–7 ounces Gruyère, Emmental,
or Beaufort cheese, grated

This is one of those dishes for which you really have to make
your own stock. Or buy some good stuff from the butcher.
There's nowhere for bad ingredients to hide. The onions
are easy enough to cook (although be prepared to keep
a constant eye on them for up to 3 hours . . . this requires
concentration rather than any real skill), but good stock
provides the depth. My wife sometimes complains that the
3-hour caramelized onions are a little too sweet. She has
a point: this is a dish to be served in starter-size portions,
otherwise it can overwhelm. As it takes so long, it makes
sense to make a big batch. Any leftovers can be frozen for
another night.

Melt the butter in a heavy saucepan over a medium–high
heat and add the onions and a big pinch of salt. Once they
are bubbling away, turn the heat right down to very low and
cook for 2–3 hours. Have faith. They'll start off milky and
drab, but check and stir every 10 or so minutes and try not
to let them burn at all. As the time passes, they'll take on
a deep golden hue.

Stir in the flour, then deglaze the pan with the wine and
vinegar. Add the thyme, hot stock, and black pepper, and
cook gently for around 1 hour.

Meanwhile, preheat the oven to 350°F. Just before serving,
put the baguette slices on a baking sheet, sprinkle with olive
oil and salt, and bake until crisp. Preheat the broiler to high.
Cover the baguette slices with cheese. Place them under the
broiler until just burnished and bubbling. Ladle the soup into
bowls and serve with the cheesy baguette.

Cauliflower cheese

1 large cauliflower

sea salt

2⅛ cups full-fat milk

1 small onion, finely chopped

2 whole cloves

1 bay leaf

4 tablespoons (½ stick) unsalted
   butter

⅓ cup all-purpose flour

7 ounces good strong
   Cheddar, grated

pinch of freshly grated nutmeg

¼ teaspoon cayenne pepper

1 teaspoon English mustard
   powder

For the tomato salad

2 tomatoes

sea salt and freshly ground
   black pepper

½ red onion, thinly sliced

extra-virgin olive oil, for drizzling

red wine vinegar, for sprinkling

I used to dread this as a child at school. Actually, I dreaded all school food, save those strange reconstituted pork ribs, garish red and shaped like a chocolate bar. Those were OK. But the cauliflower cheese. . . ugh. An overcooked, watery mass drowning in a bland white sauce thick with uncooked flour and the meanest pinch of sweaty block Cheddar. The sauce would congeal on the plate, with a wretched, translucent moat around it. This is the exact opposite: a generous, hearty, and deeply flavoured delight with a subtle tang of heat. The tomato salad offers a pert, sharp foil to all that dairy glory. It's an unlikely but perfect partner.

Remove and discard the green leaves from the cauliflower, then break into even-size florets. Cook in a pan of salted boiling water for 8–10 minutes, or until nearly tender. Drain and lay out on a folded tea towel to absorb excess moisture.

Put the milk in a saucepan, add the onion, cloves, and bay leaf, and bring to a simmer. Cook for 1–2 minutes, then cover and remove from the heat. Set aside to infuse for 10 minutes, then strain the milk through a sieve into a large measuring cup.

In another saucepan, melt the butter over a low heat and stir in the flour, making sure there are no lumps in the mixture. Cook, stirring, for a few minutes, then remove from the heat.

Pour in the milk, whisking vigorously until smooth and well combined. Return the pan to a low heat and, using a wooden spoon, stir until the sauce thickens enough to coat the back of the spoon. Leave to cook for 2–3 minutes more over the lowest heat. Preheat the oven to 375°F.

Add three-quarters of the cheese to the sauce and stir until it melts. Season with nutmeg, cayenne, mustard powder, and sea salt. Arrange the cauliflower in a shallow ovenproof dish, pour over the hot sauce, and sprinkle with the remaining cheese. Bake for 20 minutes, until the cheese is golden and the sauce is bubbling.

Meanwhile, for the salad, slice the tomatoes, place them in a serving dish, and season. Add the red onion, then drizzle with the olive oil and sprinkle lightly with the red wine vinegar. Serve alongside the cauliflower cheese.

Porcini risotto

{ SERVES 4 }

4 tablespoons (½ stick) unsalted
   butter, plus 2 tablespoons
   (¼ stick) cut into small cubes
   and kept in the fridge
1 small onion, very finely
   chopped
1½ cups carnaroli or arborio rice
   (or *vialone nano*, although this
   is more traditionally used for
   seafood risottos)
scant 1 cup dry white wine
1 ounce dried porcini
   mushrooms, soaked in
   boiling water to cover for 25
   minutes, then chopped
1 quart good chicken stock (see
   page 39), kept at a rolling boil
1 ounce Parmesan, finely grated
sea salt and freshly ground
   black pepper

Risotto does require a little patience, but no superhuman culinary technique. If you can soften an onion and stir, you'll be fine. I was taught how to make it by the great Antonio Carluccio, cigarette in one hand and glass of red in the other. Occasionally, he removed one or the other and gave the pot a stir. I'm also indebted to Giorgio Locatelli, whose recipe I've sort of adapted below. (If "adapted" is the right word; the recipes for risotto vary little from book to book.)

It's a very meditative process, with Planet Rock riffing in the background, and a glass of wine close at hand. In that ghastly therapy speak, "me time." As ever, try to get all your prep done before you start cooking: the butter cubed and put in the fridge, the cheese grated, and the mushrooms soaked. If you're feeling massively cashed up and you're making this between about November and early January, grate fresh white Alba truffle over the top. This beauty is all about the scent—deep, musty, and slightly filthy—rather than the flavour.

Heat the butter in a large, heavy-bottomed saucepan over a low heat. Add the onion and cook to soften for about 10 minutes, stirring from time to time. Add the rice and cook, stirring, for about 5 minutes, until it is white and glistening. Add the wine and cook off the alcohol for a couple of minutes. Add the mushrooms and soaking liquid.

Add a ladle of hot stock and cook over medium–high heat, stirring almost constantly, until the liquid is absorbed. Repeat again and again, only adding more stock when the rice has soaked up the last lot. After 20–25 minutes the rice should be soft yet firm, with a slight grain of crunch in the middle. Every grain should be separately definable in the mouth, yet surge together as one in the pan. Take off the heat and leave to sit for a minute. Throw in the cold butter cubes and beat the hell out of the risotto with a wooden spoon, shaking the pan until all the butter is incorporated. Add the Parmesan and do the same. Season. Serve at once.

Lemon risotto

"Oh God," I thought, when I heard this was appearing for lunch. It was our first day at a villa in Sicily, and the first thing we tried from our Tunisian cook, Naima. Lemon risotto sounded all wrong: both oversweet and cloying. What appeared was a dish so perfect that we ate in stunned silence. That the rice was cooked perfectly was a given, she was a magical cook, but the lemon just sharpened the edges, lifted the dish up, while a touch of chilli gave heat. After devouring a few platefuls, I tried to write down the recipe. Naima was secretive at first, but did admit she used vegetable rather than chicken stock. How the hell could she get that much flavour from mere vegetable stock? Anyway, as the fortnight progressed, we all fell in love with Naima and her cooking. She was a master, peerless. I never did get the exact recipe, but this comes close, gleaned from many a furtive trip into the kitchen as she was whipping it up.

{ SERVES 4 }

2 tablespoons olive oil

2 tablespoons (¼ stick) unsalted butter, plus 2 tablespoons (¼ stick) cut into small cubes and kept in the fridge

1 onion, finely chopped

2 carrots, finely chopped

2 celery stalks, finely chopped

1½ cups carnaroli or arborio rice (or *vialone nano*, although this is more traditionally used for seafood risottos)

½ cup brandy

1 quart fresh vegetable or chicken stock, kept at a rolling boil

juice and finely grated zest of 1 unwaxed lemon

1 ounce Parmesan, finely grated, plus extra to serve

sea salt and freshly ground black pepper

Heat the olive oil and 2 tablespoons of the butter in a large, heavy-bottomed saucepan over a medium heat. Add the onion, carrots, and celery and cook to soften for about 10 minutes, stirring from time to time. Add the rice and cook, stirring, until it is white and glistening, 4–5 minutes. Add the brandy and cook off the alcohol for a couple of minutes.

Add a ladle of hot stock and cook over a medium–high heat, stirring almost constantly, until all the liquid is absorbed. Repeat again and again, only adding more stock when the rice has soaked up the last lot. After about 20–25 minutes the rice should be soft yet firm, with a slight grain of crunch in the middle. Every grain should be separately definable in the mouth, yet somehow surge together as one in the pan.

Add the lemon zest and mix well. Take off the heat and leave to sit for a minute. Add the lemon juice, cold butter, and Parmesan, beating hard and banging the pot around. Season and serve with more Parmesan.

Triple-cooked chips

{ SERVES 4 }

2¾ pounds floury potatoes, such
    as Idaho, peeled
1 quart peanut oil
1 quart beef dripping or
    rendered animal fat (optional)
sea salt

I won't lie. Good chips (french fries) are a bear to make.
They involve three different stages and a quantity of boiling-
hot oil. Not a problem in itself (although I still shiver when
remembering those government adverts of my youth, where
some poor, unsuspecting fool would throw water on their
deep-fat fryer . . . with predictably horrific results), but
cooking fries does tend to make the house reek of fat. My
wife actually bans me from doing it inside. So I have to sit
outside, frying away al fresco.

    As with roast potatoes, the choice of potato is
paramount. You want a floury or mealy variety because
they concentrate a greater amount of dry starch in their
cells. During the cooking process, these cells puff and
separate, producing the dry, fluffy texture that is so
essential. I like a Maris Piper or King Edward, but the likes
of Golden Wonder, Croft, or Idaho are equally well suited.
As for the frying oil, nothing beats decent beef dripping for
the third cooking. It reaches a high heat without smoking
and adds the most wonderful flavour. Chip masters in the
north of England have long sworn by it. Peanut oil is an
acceptable alternative, but you do miss out on that extra
meaty edge.

    The two-stage frying method produces decent fries:
a lower heat to cook the center, followed by a higher one
to crisp it all up. But better still is Heston Blumenthal's
method. He's not only an incredible cook, but a gentleman,
too. Anyway, he takes the three-times-cooked approach and
it's excellent. In fact, "triple-cooked chips" are now
ubiquitous in gastro-pubs across the Britain. It all started
with Heston. I've adapted the recipe a little for added ease.

Wash the potatoes and cut into rectangular blocks, then into fries, 1½ inch thick.

Put the fries into a bowl of cold water for 10 minutes, changing the water twice to rinse off some of the starch. Drain well.

Bring a big pot of water to a boil and add the fries. Bring back to a boil and simmer gently (do not boil hard) for 4–5 minutes until almost cooked. Using a slotted spoon, lift the fries out of the water and place on a cooling rack over a roasting pan. Allow to steam dry and, when cool, place in the fridge for 20 minutes.

In a deep-fat fryer, heat the peanut oil to 270°F and plunge in the fries. After a while, they will take on a drier appearance. Do not let them brown at all. This takes about 5–8 minutes. Drain, let them cool, then put them back in the fridge for 20 minutes.

For the second frying stage, heat the rendered fat or dripping (or reheat the peanut oil if you must) to 350°F in a deep-fat fryer. Plunge in the fries and cook until golden brown. This takes 8–10 minutes. Be patient in order to obtain a really crisp fry. Drain and season with salt. Serve immediately.

Roast potatoes

{ SERVES 6 }

3 pounds floury potatoes,
   peeled
sea salt
about 6 tablespoons goose fat
   or duck fat

Here's a subject to get everyone all aquiver. On the one hand, there are those who claim they cannot make a decent roast potato, whatever method they use. On the other, there are people who decree that their's is the only way. I sit somewhere in the middle. The two main points are these: for proper, fluffy-centered beauties with a crisp, burnished crust, you need floury potatoes such as King Edward, Romano, Desiree, or Idaho. The waxy varieties are quite unsuited to the task. You also need to roughen up the edges after boiling, but before roasting. This gives that crunchy edge. As to fat, everyone will tell you different: lard/dripping/olive oil/goose fat/duck fat. I use the last two. They have a high burning point (i.e. they don't burn and get bitter in the oven) and a great flavour.

Preheat the oven to 425°F. Cut the potatoes into irregular, but same "size-ish" shapes (uniformity is boring—no one wants identical potatoes—rather some big, some slightly smaller and very crunchy, with lots of those bits you scrape from the pan).

Throw them into a big saucepan and fill with water, adding a little salt. Bring to the boil and simmer for about 10 minutes, until the outsides are a little fluffy. A knife should pass easily through the cooked potato. Chef Rowley Leigh once gave me a fine bit of advice: "Boil them as long as you dare." You obviously don't want to end up with potato broth, but a few errant scraps are always welcome. Drain and leave to steam dry for about 10–15 minutes.

Once the potatoes are dryish, give the strainer a good old rattle, so the edges of the potatoes thump together and the exteriors roughen up. Put the fat in a roasting tin and heat in the oven for 5 minutes.

When the fat is sizzling and shimmering, remove the pan from the oven, chuck in the potatoes and, using a spoon, roll them about so every surface is covered in hot fat. Put into the oven and leave for 30 minutes. Have faith. Then take out and turn and cook for another 20 minutes. By now you can start treating each potato as an individual, turning as need be. They should be done within the hour, but instead of worrying about what the recipe says, just try them. Then you'll know for sure. Season with salt and serve immediately.

Aligot

{ SERVES 4 }

2¼ pounds small–medium floury
   potatoes, such as Idaho
sea salt and freshly ground
   black pepper
2 large garlic cloves
½ cup heavy cream
5 tablespoons (½ stick plus
   1 tablespoon) unsalted butter
10½ ounces *tomme de Cantal*
   cheese, cut into very thin
   slices, or grated Caerphilly
   or Lancashire
hot milk, for mixing, if needed

Mashed potato and cheese. Whipped together. There's
no doubting its primal allure. You do really need *tomme
de Cantal,* a soft, young white French cheese, for this recipe.
You could substitute grated Caerphilly or a Lancashire (Mrs.
Kirkham's is the best), but then it would be cheesy mashed
potato rather than *aligot*. Which is no bad thing, either.

Boil the potatoes in their skins until tender: about 15–25
minutes, depending on size. Remove the skins and push
the potato flesh through a sieve to achieve a dry purée.
Season to taste with salt and pepper.

In a small bowl, crush the garlic with a little salt to soften.

Put the cream and butter in a heavy saucepan and heat
until the butter melts. Add the potato and stir until
thoroughly combined. Add the garlic. Stir in the cheese
all at once, and beat vigorously until the mixture becomes
smooth and elastic. It should pull into bubble gum-like
strings when you lift the spoon; if the mixture is too stiff,
add a little hot milk. Serve immediately.

Sprouts in stock

Brussels sprouts are more sinned against than sinning. It's often the memories of school food that taint these magnificent vegetables. Cooked to buggery, until soggy and sulphurous, they're foul. Treated with respect, though, they transform from dowdy lumps into fresh-faced beauties. This recipe is quick, easy, and guaranteed to transform the most dyed-in-the-wool sprout abuser to instant obsessive.

Heat the butter in a frying pan until foaming, then add the sprouts and cook gently for 5 minutes.

Add the hot stock, enough to cover the sprouts to not quite halfway, and the thyme and cook for another 5 minutes until it forms a sort of thin glaze on the vegetables. Add a shake of Tabasco, a squeeze of lemon juice, and salt and pepper to taste. Serve at once.

{ SERVES 4 }

2 tablespoons (¼ stick) unsalted butter

1⅛ pounds Brussels sprouts, outer leaves removed, cut into ¼-inch-thick rounds

1 cup hot chicken stock (cube OK, fresh better)

big pinch of thyme leaves

Tabasco sauce

juice of ½ lemon

sea salt and freshly ground black pepper

Sticky toffee pudding

{ SERVES 6 }

4 tablespoons (½ stick) unsalted
   butter, softened, plus extra to
   butter the dish
6 ounces dates, chopped
1 teaspoon baking soda
¾ cup plus 2½ tablespoons
   superfine sugar
2 eggs
1¼ cups self-rising flour
1 teaspoon vanilla extract
vanilla ice cream, to serve

For the sauce
1¼ cups heavy cream
¼ cup demerara sugar
1½ teaspoons black treacle

Not so long ago, I imagined this pudding as an old English classic (well, at least dating back to the time when sugar made it to our shores), devoured by Tristram Shandy, Daniel Deronda, and David Copperfield in his dotage. Yet this is a relatively recent invention. Despite claims to the contrary, STP was not first conjured up by The Village Shop in Cartmel—although this is one of the best you can buy. But, according to Jane Grigson, by Francis Coulson of Sharrow Bay on Ullswater in the Lake District. There, the story goes, he came up with the original recipe that has been copied ever since. Even this, though, is open to conjecture. Chef Simon Hopkinson recalls Coulson's admission, over a typically splendid dinner, that "There was this sweet woman in Lancashire . . . and such a lovely cook . . . Marvellous puddings! And, well, yes . . . there might have been a recipe published somewhere . . . But mine is much better, and we call our updated version the 'Icky-Sticky Toffee Sponge' to avoid any confusion!"

So perhaps the original recipe came from a Mrs. Martin. A few years later, her son, Piers, contacted Simon to relay the origins of his mother's dish. Far from being some great national pudding, she actually got her recipe from a Canadian friend. The horror! Still, the British have quickly made it their own and the debate as to its roots detracts nothing from the utter beauty of this pudding. Don't scrimp on the sauce, and please: no nuts or slivers of peel, no chunks of chocolate, or glugs of brandy. Sticky Toffee Pudding needs no embellishments. This is certainly not my take on the recipe. Just the original recipe, in all its glory. Don't mess with perfection.

{ CONTINUES OVERLEAF }

Preheat the oven to 350°F. Butter a baking pan about 8 x 5 inches.

Boil the dates in 1¼ cups water until soft (some dates are softer than others, so will need more cooking), then remove the pan from the heat and drain any liquid. Add the baking soda.

Cream the butter and sugar together until light and fluffy, then add the eggs and beat well. Mix in the flour, date mixture, and vanilla extract and pour into the prepared pan. Bake for 30–40 minutes, until just firm to the touch.

To make the sauce, boil the cream, sugar, and treacle together. Pour over the top of the sponge until it is covered (there will be some left over), then place under a hot broiler until it begins to bubble. Remove, cut into squares, and serve with the remaining sauce and a scoop of vanilla ice cream.

Trifle

Is there any dish less suited to its name than trifle? This glorious spectacle of a pudding is neither slight nor trivial. Or frivolous either. It requires hard work (baking the sponge, making the custard) and dedication. And it's miles removed from the school version, a sorry travesty and depressing mix of tinned fruit and lurid yellow custard (mixed from custard powder). Trifle has a long history, starting out as the bastard child of tipsy cake (sponge bathed in booze) and basic custard, little more than almond milk. Over time, the two dishes melded by way of a thickened, spiced cream to create this buxom queen of the festive table. It was a dish for the rich (good ones always were; the poor made do on scraps and gruel), but there's no authentic version. Aside from making everything fresh, a huge glass bowl is essential to show off all those lovely layers. If you are artistically inclined, the top of a trifle is a blank canvas on which to indulge your most outrageous candied fruit and petalled whims.

First, make the sponge. Preheat the oven to 350°F. Butter a 6-inch round cake pan and line with parchment paper. Beat all the sponge ingredients together in a mixing bowl until smooth. Spoon into the pan, level the surface, and bake for 20 minutes, or until lightly golden, well risen, and the top springs back when lightly pressed with a fingertip. Leave to cool in the pan, then loosen the edges and turn out onto a wire rack to cool completely.

{ CONTINUES OVERLEAF }

{ SERVES 6 }

For the sponge

2 tablespoons unsalted butter, softened, plus extra to butter the dish

¼ cup superfine sugar

1 large egg, lightly beaten

⅓ cup self-rising flour, sifted

For the custard

2½ cups light cream

1 vanilla bean, split lengthwise

3 eggs

4 egg yolks

¼ cup superfine sugar, plus extra for sprinkling

2 level teaspoons cornstarch

For the layers

1 (5-ounce) strawberry gelatin tablet

¼ cup fino sherry

12 ounces raspberries

1¼ cups heavy cream

2 (1½-ounce) Crunchie bars, roughly chopped

2 tablespoons flaked almonds, toasted

To make the custard, put the cream into a saucepan with the vanilla bean and heat slowly, until it reaches boiling point. Let to stand for 10–15 minutes to allow the flavours to develop. Remove the vanilla bean, scrape out the seeds, and add to the cream. Discard the pod.

In a bowl, whisk the eggs, yolks, sugar, and cornstarch together until well mixed. Reheat the cream, then gradually whisk it into the egg mixture until smooth, using a balloon whisk. Return the mixture to the pan over a medium–low heat, stirring gently until thick. Put it into a bowl, whisk again, then sprinkle the surface with a little extra sugar or cover with a piece of crumpled and wetted nonstick parchment paper to prevent a skin from forming. Cover and transfer to the fridge to chill well.

Make up the gelatin as directed on the package, then allow it to cool. Slice the sponge and arrange it in the base of a 2½-quart glass bowl. Douse in sherry until wet but not soggy. Top with a good layer of raspberries, keeping a few to decorate. Pour in the liquid jelly, cover, and leave in the fridge to set.

Spoon the custard over the set gelatin. Whisk the cream until it form soft swirls, then fold in two-thirds of the chopped candy. Spoon the cream over the custard and leave as soft waves. Sprinkle with the remaining chopped candy, raspberries, and the flaked almonds. Chill until ready to serve.

Treacle tart

{ SERVES 4–6 }

8 ounces shortcrust pastry

a little all-purpose flour, for
   dusting

butter, for greasing

2 ounces white bread, a couple
   of days old, crusts removed

1 cup golden syrup

juice of ½ small lemon

large pinch of ground ginger

1 small egg, beaten (optional)

A fine pudding, and one improved immeasurably by a hint of ginger and a squeeze of lemon juice. This was my favourite pudding when I was young, cooked by the brilliant Bridget, an immaculately coiffed cook with the most generous of bosoms. She made the finest treacle tart I ever tasted. This recipe is not my own, or even Bridget's, but is based on one taken from a classic pudding tome: the late Mary Norwak's *English Puddings, Sweet & Savoury* (Grub Street, 2004).

Preheat the oven to 350°F. Roll out the pastry on a lightly floured surface and use it to line a 8–9-inch greased pie plate.

Tear the bread into small pieces and blitz in a food processor to make fine crumbs.

Gently warm the golden syrup and lemon juice in a saucepan, then stir in the breadcrumbs and ginger. Tip the mixture into the pastry shell and spread evenly. Brush the edge of the pastry lightly and evenly with beaten egg if you wish. Bake for 20–25 minutes, until the pastry is golden. Serve hot or cold with cream.

Eccles cakes

{MAKES 12 –14}

For the pastry

1¾ cups all-purpose flour, sifted,
   plus extra for rolling out pastry
pinch of salt
12 tablespoons (1½ sticks) cold
   unsalted butter, divided into 4
   pieces
milk, to glaze

For the filling

4 ounces dried currants
1 rounded tablespoon superfine
   sugar, plus extra for glazing
large pinch of freshly grated
   nutmeg
3 tablespoons unsalted butter

The late Winnie Swarbrick was a magnificent lady and an incredible baker. Her ginger cakes, butter biscuits, and chocolate cake, cooked in her small Goosnargh kitchen, are seared in my memory. And her Eccles cakes were the best in the world. She died last year, and is much missed.

To make the pastry, mix the flour and salt in a bowl, then rub a quarter of the butter into the flour. Add just enough water to form an elastic dough. Turn this out onto a lightly floured surface and use a rolling pin to roll it out into a rectangular strip about 6 x 14 inches. Brush off any surplus flour.

Chop another quarter of the butter into cubes and dot it evenly over two-thirds of the pastry rectangle. Fold the pastry into thirds, bringing the end without fat to the center, then folding over the other third. Press the pastry edges together with your fingers or a rolling pin, give the pastry a quarter turn so the folds are left and right, and roll out lightly. Cover and let rest in the fridge for an hour, then repeat the process of dotting with butter, folding, and rolling twice more, resting the pastry for an hour time.

While the pastry chills, make the filling. Mix the currants and sugar together, then add the nutmeg. While you are doing this, melt the butter. Pour the melted butter into the currant mixture and stir, then set aside to cool. Preheat the oven to 350°F.

Roll out the pastry until it is ¼ inch thick, then cut out 12 circles with a 2¾-inch round cutter. Place a dessertspoon (about 1½ teaspoons) of the cooled currant mixture in the center of each circle and draw the edges of pastry together. Turn the pastry over, smooth side up, and then roll lightly to flatten. Place on a lightly greased baking sheet.

Make 3 cuts in the top to show the filling, brush with milk, and sprinkle with superfine sugar. Bake for 15–20 minutes (check after 15 minutes), until golden.

Eccles cake ice cream

**{ MAKES ABOUT 800 ML/
1½ PINTS }**

1⅔ cups full-fat milk

1 vanilla bean, split lengthwise

½ cup unrefined granulated
  sugar

4 egg yolks

1 cup heavy cream

4 Eccles cakes (see recipe on
  page 80), torn to small shreds

I came up with this recipe when food writer Matthew Fort and I were invited to cook a dinner for that fine northern chef, Nigel Haworth, at Northcote Manor in Lancashire. I say "cook", but we didn't do much of the hard graft, instead poncing about in chef's whites, marvelling at the professionalism and work of his 20-person brigade. Still, this recipe, combining classic French vanilla ice cream (based on a recipe in Caroline and Robin Weir's masterwork, *Ice Creams, Sorbets & Gelati: The Definitive Guide*, Grub Street, 2010) with these baked northern beauties, went down well. Even if the nearest thing I did to work was adding a sprig of something or other to the plate at the end. Some things are best left to the pros.

Combine the milk, vanilla bean, and half the sugar in a saucepan and bring to a boil. Remove from the heat and set aside for 20 minutes. In a heatproof bowl, combine the egg yolks with the remaining sugar and beat with an electric whisk (or by hand, if you're feeling particularly energetic) until thick. Remove the vanilla bean from the milk, scrape out the seeds into the milk, and discard the pod.

Bring the milk back to boiling point and then, whisking steadily, pour it in a slow, thin stream, into the yolks and sugar. Place the bowl over a pan of simmering water and stir with a spatula for about 15 minutes, until thick and smooth; the mixture should coat the back of the spatula. Cool the bowl by plunging the bottom into cold water, and leave the custard to cool.

Add the cream and stir. Put into an ice cream machine and churn for 25 minutes, or according to the manufacturer's instructions. Add the Eccles cake pieces 5 minutes before the end of the churning time. Serve straight from the machine or transfer to a plastic container and put in the freezer.

Rhubarb & ginger crumble

I'm not a pastry man. A maker of the stuff, I mean, rather than an eater, which I most certainly am. Too much precision needed, and patience, too. But crumble is different. Pinching sugar and flour into butter is always a soothing pleasure—just like the dish itself. It's actually a relatively modern invention, born from the strictures of rationing in World War II. Normal pastry used too much rare and precious flour, so someone came up with crumble. You don't want the topping too thick: no more than half an inch. It should flatter and add contrast to the soft filling, not overwhelm it.

Preheat the oven to 350°F. Melt the butter in a saucepan, add the rhubarb, sugar, and grated ginger and cook until soft, about 5 minutes. Put into a shallow 1-quart ovenproof dish.

To make the crumble, put the flour, butter, and ground ginger into a bowl, and rub the butter into the flour until it resembles coarse breadcrumbs. Stir in half the sugar. Spread the crumble over the fruit and scatter with the remaining sugar. Bake for 45 minutes, or until the top is crisp and golden. Serve with cream or vanilla ice cream.

{ SERVES 4 }

1 tablespoon unsalted butter
1½ pounds rhubarb, cut into 2-inch lengths
½ cup plus 1 tablespoon light brown sugar
1 (¾-inch) piece fresh ginger, peeled and grated
heavy cream or vanilla ice cream, to serve

For the crumble topping
1½ cups all-purpose flour
7 tablespoons (¾ stick plus 1 tablespoon) cold unsalted butter, diced
pinch of ground ginger
¼ cup demerara sugar

Autumn pudding

{ SERVES 6 }

1 pound ripe plums
1 pound ripe blackberries
½ pound red currants
  or white currants
½ cup superfine sugar
1 medium white loaf bread
heavy cream, to serve

This juice-stained beauty was originally known as "hydropathic pudding," a rather clinical, dour name for such a splendid confection. But as it contained no pastry, it was seen as the sort of thing well suited to the diet of a spa. So after the enema, Scotch hose, and Swiss shower, I'm pretty sure that this would come as sweet relief. I've changed the summer pudding to an autumn one, because I think all those blackberries, plums, and red currants work even better than raspberries. The key is a balance of the sweet and tart. Use good bread, too. The cheap stuff, fine as it is for bacon sandwiches, tends to become slimy.

Wash the fruit and remove the stones, stalks, and strings. Quarter the plums and put them in a saucepan with the sugar and ½ cup water. Bring to the boil, then simmer gently for 5 minutes. Add the blackberries, cook for 3 minutes, then add the currants and cook for 3 minutes more, stirring from time to time, until the fruit is tender but keeps its shape. Allow to cool slightly.

Line a 1½-quart pudding bowl with 2 long pieces of plastic wrap so the base and sides are lined and the plastic wrap drapes over the top edges of the bowl. Cut the loaf into ½-inch-thick slices, then, using 8–9 slices depending on the size of the loaf, trim off the crusts. Cut a circle the size of the base of the bowl, add to the bowl, then cut 5–6 slices of bread in half and arrange around the sides of the bowl, overlapping the edges slightly and pressing together.

Spoon in the warm fruit, reserving a little juice for serving, and cover with the remaining bread, again pressing the edges together. Fold the plastic wrap over the top, cover with a small plate, and weigh down with 2 cans of food. Put in the fridge overnight. Cover with a serving plate, invert the bowl, then remove it. Peel off the plastic wrap and brush any white patches with the reserved juice. Serve with lashings of cream.

Chocolate & orange soufflés

{ SERVES 6 }

3 tablespoons unsalted butter, at room temperature

6 tablespoons superfine sugar

3 large eggs, separated

4 level teaspoons cornstarch

4 level teaspoons all-purpose flour

2 level teaspoons cocoa powder

1 cup full-fat milk

5½ ounces dark chocolate, broken into pieces

grated rind of 1 medium orange

2 tablespoons orange juice

a little confectioners' sugar, sifted, to decorate

Don't fear soufflés. They're very easy, despite what you might think. The key is to get air into your mixture, so it rises in the oven. And fold in the egg whites slowly, not fast as many recommend. Harold McGee, scientist and author of *On Food and Cooking* (1984), agrees, arguing that fast mixing will damage the foam. And what he says goes.

Preheat the oven to 375°F. Generously butter the inside of six ⅔-cup ovenproof ramekins right up to the top, reserving the remaining butter. Sprinkle 2 tablespoons of the sugar into the ramekins, tilt to cover the insides with the sugar, then tip out the excess. Put the ramekins on a baking sheet.

Whisk the egg yolks and remaining 4 tablespoons sugar in a bowl for a few minutes until thick and pale. Sift in the flours and cocoa, then mix briefly until smooth.

Pour the milk into a saucepan, bring to a boil, then gradually whisk into the egg mixture. Return to the pan and cook over a medium heat, stirring constantly, until thick and smooth. Take off the heat and add the chocolate and remaining butter, leave for a minute until melted, then stir in the orange rind and juice. Leave to cool for 10 minutes.

Whisk the egg whites in a large clean glass bowl to soft peaks. Fold a spoonful into the chocolate mixture to loosen it, then gently fold in the remaining whites. Divide among the ramekins, run a finger around the edges, then bake for 12–15 minutes, until risen above the top of the ramekins with a slight wobble in the center. Dust with sifted confectioners' sugar.

{ Quick fixes }

In a perfect world, we'd all cook every night, spending hours slaving over the stove to create dishes that would excite even the most leaden of palates. But after a long, dreary day at work, the last thing you usually want to do is slice a dozen carrots, brown meat, and skim broth. You want to eat, and fast. I'd be a liar if I didn't admit to the odd (or not so odd) takeaway, as well as wrapping hastily torn chunks of cheese in pre-sliced white bread. Or eating ham by the fistful, straight from the package. These are the quickest fixes of all, though they tend not to endear one to one's better half. The recipes in this section are a touch more civilized; they're all about ease and speed. Some may take longer than 30 minutes to marinate and cook, but none need more than 15 minutes (and that's 15 amateur minutes, not 15 of Marcus Wareing's or Jason Atherton's minutes) to prepare. And compared to the ghastly ready meal, these dishes will thrill and delight.

{ Steak }

There's no bore worse than a steak bore. Give them the chance, and they'll bang on for days, with all the spittle-specked, bright-eyed enthusiasm of a Jehovah's Witness going door-to-door. Eyes glaze over as they describe that hunk of 54-day-aged Belted Galloway they once ate in a steakhouse so exclusive that only the seventh son of a seventh son has a chance of being admitted through its hallowed doors. Or the sliver of sirloin chopped from a cow that was raised by virgins and that supped on the spring of eternal youth.

But really, the world is awash with average steak, the stuff that looks OK, tastes OK, but hardly lingers in the memory. Add a little butter, gravy, or sauce and things improve. But truly great steak is a rare beast. Its creation is as much art as science.

Good breeding is not enough. Pure Angus, Longhorn, and Devon Red are all wonderful native British breeds. But without the right feed (and grass is always best, with a little winter silage) or with amateur finishing (the process towards the end of a cow's life where the protein in feed is increased to create a good, hard layer of fat), you may as well be cutting into American feedlot pap. Then there's the age (older means more flavour), the slaughter (as stress-free as possible), the hanging, and the butchering. Muck up one stage and the whole thing's a busted flush.

Your choice of cut can help. None are better than the others, just different. Filet or tenderloin is the most tender, as it has the least work to do when the animal is alive. Think of it as the dissolute but vacuous toff: fun every now and then, but can grate rather quickly. All that indolence makes for little depth. Sirloin is more middle-class in its work ethic, sitting above the fillet or tenderloin and taking part in light, white-collar labour. So it mixes pleasing texture with the prospect of taste. The rump is resolutely working class, a cut that has to toil for a living, shifting the hind legs and supporting the butt. The result—plenty of chew and, hopefully, character, too. These, of course, are outlines painted with the broadest of strokes. Good fillet or tenderloin can possess far more depth than run-of-the-mill rump. And humble skirt, sliced from a well-brought-up cow, will delight rather more than prime rib chopped from a bore.

As to cooking, unless you possess a professional grill that burns hotter than Hades, a heavy cast-iron griddle pan is best. Heat it over a high heat for at least 10 minutes. Then oil your steak (not the pan) and season with a heavy hand. For rare, I cook each side for 2 minutes and rest for 4. For medium, go for 3 minutes and rest for 6. For well done . . . well, as long as you want. The taste and texture would have left the building after 5 minutes on each side anyway.

'Truly great steak is a rare beast. Its creation is as much art as science.

Good breeding is not enough.'

Steak

{ SERVES 2 }

2 (9–10-ounce) sirloin steaks,
  about 2 inches thick
peanut or olive oil
sea salt and freshly ground
  black pepper
green salad, to serve

Let the steaks come to room temperature, covered. Heat a cast-iron griddle pan over a high heat for 10 minutes, until smoking.

Massage the steaks with oil and season with a heavy hand: lots of salt and generous with the pepper, too.

Place the steaks in the pan and *don't touch for 2 minutes.* No poking, prodding, or general mucking about. Then turn them over and repeat. (For medium steaks, cook for 3 minutes on each side.)

When time's up, remove to a warmed plate and rest for 4 minutes (6 minutes for medium). Serve with a crisp green salad.

Asian steak in lettuce

I once had to taste thirty steaks in a day. Being fundamentally greedy, I couldn't just take a slice of each. I started at a sprint, wolfing down great slabs of the first half-dozen. The pace did slow and, by the end, even thinking became vexed. I could barely move. Anyway, the next day saw my fridge filled with cold, cooked steak. So in a desperate bid to inject some greenery into my swollen, stolid gut, I sliced up the steak, covered it with herbs and cucumber, wrapped it in lettuce, and dipped it in a fiery, lime-spiked fish sauce. Bliss, and it could even be described as healthy. Well, healthy*ish*, anyway.

Slice the steaks thinly across the grain and lay them on a plate. On separate plates, lay out the lettuce leaves, herbs, and cucumber. Mix all the sauce ingredients together and put into a bowl.

To serve, take some steak, cup it in a lettuce leaf, cover in herbs and cucumber, wrap, and dip in sauce. Repeat at will.

{ SERVES 4 AS A STARTER }

2 (9–10-ounce) steaks, cooked (see page 92)
2 soft lettuces, leaves separated
handful of cilantro, roughly chopped
handful of mint, roughly chopped
1 cucumber, cut into slivers

For the dipping sauce
6 tablespoons fresh lime
3 tablespoons fish sauce
5–10 bird's-eye chillies, chopped

Peas with pancetta

{ SERVES 4 }

¼ cup extra-virgin olive oil

3½ ounces unsmoked pancetta,
   finely chopped

½ small onion, finely chopped

½ cup dry white wine
   (Verdicchio, if possible)

3 pounds fresh peas, shelled,
   or scant 1 pound shelled peas

Fresh peas have a sweetness that is impossible to match. But frozen peas are fine here, too. If you can't find pancetta, substitute bacon. This is a steadfast side dish.

Heat the oil in a large sauté pan over a medium heat and cook the pancetta until crisp and golden. Add the onion and sauté for 5 minutes, stirring frequently.

Add the wine, reduce the heat to medium-hot, and simmer gently for a few minutes to reduce slightly. When the onion begins to soften, add the peas and cook for 2 minutes more, stirring continuously. Serve immediately.

Spaghetti alla carbonara

{ SERVES 2 }

9 ounces good smoked pancetta
   or smoked streaky bacon,
   diced
1 garlic clove, lightly bruised
12 ounces spaghetti
sea salt and freshly ground
   black pepper
3 eggs, beaten
6 tablespoons freshly
   grated Parmesan

Forget all those horribly rich, cream-soaked aberrations they call carbonara. They usually have the texture of wallpaper paste, and sit uncomfortably in the belly for hours. This fairly proper version (and by this I mean better, not trainspotterly "authentic") depends totally on the quality of the ingredients: good, fresh eggs, and proper smoked pancetta or decent smoked streaky bacon.

Fry the pancetta or bacon with the garlic over a medium heat until crisp. Remove the garlic. Drain the pancetta and set aside.

Cook the spaghetti in lots of boiling water, with a generous amount of salt, according to package instructions. Drain.

Put the hot spaghetti into a clean warmed pan, throw over the eggs, and mix well, then add the pancetta/bacon and Parmesan, and season to taste with lots of black pepper. The egg mixture should cling to each strand but not become scrambled. Serve immediately.

Rack of lamb

This is an expensive cut, but nothing beats ripping just-pink chunks of lamb from the bone, then knawing off any last, juicy scraps. I could eat a whole rack myself, but then I'm a pig. One rack shared between two should do fine. As with all lamb, avoid the stuff that appears in early spring. It might seem traditional, but it ain't.

Preheat the oven to 425°F. Massage 1 tablespoon of the olive oil into the lamb, along with the herbs, salt, and pepper, and leave for 10 minutes.

Heat the remaining oil in a heavy roasting pan over a high heat, then brown the rack all over: fat side first for 3 minutes and bottom for 2. Put in the oven, fat side up, and cook for 15 minutes. Rest for 5 minutes before serving with a green salad and baked potatoes.

{ SERVES 2 }

1 (6-bone) rack of lamb,
  French-trimmed
2 tablespoons olive oil
handful of mixed rosemary
  and thyme, finely chopped
sea salt and freshly ground
  black pepper
green salad, to serve
baked potatoes, to serve

Griddled lamb with cucumber raita

{ SERVES 2 }

1 pound shoulder or leg of lamb,
  off the bone, fat removed
5½ ounces Greek yogurt
1 teaspoon ground coriander
pinch of ground cumin
pinch of freshly ground
  black pepper
juice of ½ lemon

**For the cucumber
  and tomato raita**
9 ounces Greek yogurt
½ cucumber, seeded and finely
  diced
4 tomatoes or 16 cherry
  tomatoes, finely chopped
2 tablespoons cilantro or mint,
  finely chopped
1 teaspoon ground cumin
sea salt and freshly ground
  black pepper

A fine summer dinner, this time with an Eastern Mediterranean scent. Despite reports to the contrary, the lamb we eat in spring is not much good. Tender, yes, but a total stranger to flavour. In the old days, spring was the time lambs were born, and they were eaten towards the end of summer, when they actually tasted of something. Even better, they were slaughtered at a year old, around hogget age. Nowadays, the market demands lamb for Easter, so we eat beasts that are born in October, and overwintered indoors, kept from those verdant shoots of sweet new grass. Hence the lack of lamby heft. Anything over a year, though, and you're looking at a tougher beast, better suited to braising than barbecuing or griddling.

Cut the lamb into 1¼-inch chunks. Mix together the yogurt, coriander, cumin, black pepper, and lemon juice in a bowl. Add the lamb, mix well, cover, and leave to sit in the fridge for at least an hour.

To make the cucumber and tomato raita, mix the yogurt, cucumber, tomatoes, herbs, and cumin together. Season to taste and chill, covered, until ready to serve. If barbecuing, get your coals good and hot.

When you are ready to cook the lamb, take it out of the marinade and season, but do not wipe off the marinade. Thread the meat onto metal skewers (or use wooden satay sticks that have been soaked in water for an hour to prevent them from catching fire).

Grill over a high heat for 8–10 minutes on the barbecue or griddle pan, turning and basting with the marinade every so often. Serve hot with the raita.

BBQ butterflied leg of lamb

{ SERVES 6 }

1 (3⅓-pound) leg of lamb,
  butterflied (ask your butcher
  to do this)
2 garlic cloves, crushed
1 teaspoon hot paprika
2 tablespoons red wine vinegar
2 teaspoons thyme leaves,
  finely chopped
1 tablespoon olive oil
green salad, to serve
crusty rolls, to serve

This is a mighty fine barbecue dish, and very easy to make. Get your butcher to butterfly the leg of lamb. When cooking, ensure the flames don't roar out of control; this isn't a Burger King advert. You want grilled meat, not scorched flesh. Rest for at least 10 minutes, then carve into thick slices.

Put the lamb in a big bowl. Mix together the garlic, paprika, vinegar, and thyme and rub into the lamb. Drizzle over the olive oil, cover, and leave to marinate in the fridge overnight (or for a minimum of 2 hours), turning occasionally.

Take the lamb out of the fridge and allow to come up to room temperature, and spark up the barbie. Wait until the flames have died down and the coals are covered with gray ash. Depending on the charcoal, this can take up to an hour.

Cook the lamb for about 10 minutes on each side (this gives a pink center; for well done give it 15 minutes on each side), or until done to your liking. Leave to rest for 10 minutes before serving. Slice the lamb and serve with a green salad and crusty rolls.

A simple dish for bachelors & widowers to impress their guests

{ SERVES 2 }

1 onion, cut into wedges

3 garlic cloves, roughly chopped

sea salt and freshly ground black pepper

3 tablespoons dry white wine or dry sherry

3 tablespoons olive oil, plus extra for the chicken

2 chicken legs and 2 chicken thighs (the best you can afford)

juice of 1 lemon

green salad, to serve

baked potatoes, to serve

My father is a serious eater, but was never much of a cook. His only real speciality when we were children was steaks grilled on the top of the Aga in a toast rack. The result was near perfect, but did tend to leave an inch of smoking, blackened fat on the stovetop. My mother was always less than impressed. He later married Rose, who really knew her stuff. When she became ill, he took over the culinary reins and became, in the months before she died, a rather good cook. He's not one for faffing about with prissy presentation, and this dish takes under 5 minutes to prepare.

Preheat the oven to 350°F. Line a roasting pan with foil. Add the onion and garlic, season, then add the wine or sherry and olive oil.

Rub the chicken with a little more olive oil and add to the pan, skin side down.

Cook for 45 minutes, or until cooked through, basting after 15 and 30 minutes. At 30 minutes, turn over the chicken legs. To check if they're cooked, poke a skewer into the thickest part of the thigh; the juices should be golden, not pink. If not, cook for a little longer, then retest.

Remove from the oven and allow to rest for 10 minutes. Sprinkle with a little more salt and the lemon juice. Serve with a green salad and baked potatoes.

Broiled Dover sole

{ SERVES 2 }

4 tablespoons (½ stick) unsalted
  butter, melted
2 (12-ounce) Dover sole,
  skinned and gutted, fins
  removed but head intact
sea salt and freshly ground
  black pepper
1 lemon, halved
buttered peas, to serve
sautéed waxy potatoes, to serve

For me, the sole is the greatest of all fish—with a price to match. That wonderful, near-gelatinous texture, the sweet, faintly uric flesh. Forget Escoffier and his 155 ways with this beautiful flatfish. You want it broiled, with butter and a good squeeze of lemon. This is a treat and demands to be served with peas and sautéed waxy potatoes.

Preheat the broiler to maximum for about 15 minutes. Line the broiler pan with foil, brush with melted butter, and put the fish on top. Paint the fish liberally with melted butter and season with salt and pepper, then cook for 4–6 minutes on one side. The tail should just start to smoulder.

Turn over and cook for another 2–3 minutes, until the flesh lifts easily off the bone. Serve with buttered peas and sautéed waxy potatoes.

Salt-baked sea bass

This is a grand, expensive, and expansive dish, requiring a whole wild sea bass and a shedload of salt. Don't waste your Maldon on this one—use the cheapest sea salt you can buy. The salt solidifies in the heat and the fish arrives at the table entombed in a hard white mound. But inside its sodium chloride prison, the fish will have steamed in its own juices, untouched by the salt. A few cracks, a careful peel, and you have the most splendidly succulent fish.

{ SERVES 4 }

2 pounds sea salt

2 egg whites

4 slices of lemon

a few sprigs of dill (not too much, as it's quite a bully)

2 bay leaves

1 (2⅛-pound) wild sea bass, scaled and gutted

Preheat the oven to 400°F. Line a roasting pan, a little larger than the fish, with foil. Mix the salt and egg whites together, then spread a thinnish layer about the shape and size of the fish on the foil. Stuff the lemon, dill, and bay into the fish's cavity, then put the fish on the salt in the pan.

Mold the rest of the salt mixture over and around the fish to enclose it, patting it into place with your hands.

Bake for 25 minutes. Crack open with the handle of a big knife, peel away the salt, and eat.

Spiced grilled mackerel

{ SERVES 4 }

4 mackerel, gutted
3 garlic cloves, crushed
1 tablespoon ground cumin
1 teaspoon ground coriander
½ teaspoon cayenne pepper
3 tablespoons olive oil
juice of ½ lemon
2 lemons, halved, to serve

Mackerel: the most underrated of fish. Cheap, sustainable, and, when fresh, utterly divine. The problem is that after a few days it turns from hero to stinking zero. If you have a barbecue, use it. Everything tastes better when cooked over hot coals.

Slash each mackerel diagonally 3 or 4 times on each side, then place them in a bowl. Mix together the garlic, spices, olive oil, and lemon juice, then rub the mixture all over the mackerel. Cover and put in the fridge to marinate for 20 minutes.

Heat a large griddle pan over a medium heat (or even better, heat a barbecue until hot, the flames have died down, and the coals glow softly). Add the mackerel and cook for 3–5 minutes on each side, or until golden brown all over and cooked through; the flesh should be opaque and flake easily. Remove from the pan and serve with lemon to squeeze over the fish.

Smoked trout & bacon hash

Everyone loves a hash. Proper, belly-filling stuff. You could use leftover potatoes here, or new ones. But high-starch is the key, so a russet is best. You want all those crispy, golden edges. You could also substitute smoked trout for smoked haddock, but poach in milk gently for 5 minutes first, then flake.

Fry the bacon until crisp. Drain on kitchen paper and set aside. Add butter to the bacon fat and heat until it foams. Add the onion and cook over low heat until soft. Raise the heat and add the potatoes, cooking until crisp and golden, about 5–10 minutes. Add the smoked trout, mix, then season and add Tabasco. Throw in the parsley. Once all wonderfully burnished, divide into two and top with a poached egg.

{ SERVES 2 }

1 onion, thinly sliced

1 lb russet (or other high-starch potato), boiled, chopped into ½ inch cubes

1 lb smoked trout (or smoked haddock), flaked

6 rashers of smoked bacon

knob of butter

big jig of Tabasco

salt and pepper

handful of fresh parsley, chopped

two eggs, poached, to serve

Kipper pâté

4 (10-ounce) good kippers

8 ounces cream cheese

big pinch of hot paprika, or to
    taste

sea salt and freshly ground
    black pepper

2 tablespoons light cream

good toast, to serve

2 lemons, quartered, to serve

The only problem with grilling a kipper, anointed with
a fat flake of butter, is that the fishy tang tends to linger.
My late stepmother Rose used to implore my father to
poach them instead. "Not a chance," he'd reply. "Totally
different taste." A good kipper is a grand thing indeed,
but for those of a more delicate constitution this classic
kipper pâté is unbeatable.

Poach the kippers in simmering water for 3–4 minutes,
then let them cool in the liquid. Remove the skin and
bones and flake.

Using a plastic spatula, or ideally a food processor, work
the cream cheese into a smooth cream, adding paprika,
salt, and black pepper to taste. Stir in the cream and then
gradually work the kipper into the mixture. When smooth,
chill, covered, for an hour. Serve with good toast and a few
quarters of lemon.

Clam fritters

Gloriously easy to make, and equally good as a snack or light supper. Or even a canapé, if you're that way inclined.

Put the clams and wine in a saucepan over a medium heat, cover tightly, and steam over a high heat for 2–3 minutes, or until the clams have opened. Discard any that fail to open.

Lift out the clams and, using a slotted spoon, take out the meat and chop finely.

Strain the remaining wine and clam juice into a clean pan and boil for 3–4 minutes to reduce by half. Taste. If too salty, leave out the salt from the batter.

To make the batter, sift the flour and salt together. Beat in the egg and add the reduced wine/clam broth. Mix until it has the consistency of porridge, then mix in the clam meat, cayenne, and chopped parsley.

Pour oil into a medium saucepan until about one-third full and heat until a little batter dropped into it bubbles immediately. Drop the fritter mixture, a teaspoon at a time, into the hot oil. Remove with a slotted spoon when nut-brown. Drain on paper towels and serve immediately.

{ MAKES ABOUT 20 }

about 50 clams, rinsed and
    scrubbed if necessary,
    discarding any open or
    broken shells
scant 1 cup dry white wine
½ cup plus 1 tablespoon all-
    purpose flour
½ teaspoon salt
1 egg, beaten
½ teaspoon cayenne pepper
handful of flat-leaf parsley, finely
    chopped
sunflower oil, for deep-frying

Marinated prawns

12 very fresh raw prawns
juice of 2 lemons
4 tablespoons extra-virgin
  olive oil
sea salt and freshly ground
  black pepper
handful of flat-leaf parsley,
  finely chopped

This dish is totally dependent on the quality and freshness of the prawns. Best of all are those Italian beauties, the *gambero rosso*, with scarlet body and the sweetest of flesh. You can use any type of prawn, as long they are uncooked, not previously frozen, and ideally just hauled from the sea. If the antennae are still on, it's a good sign, as they drop off within hours of capture.

Clean the prawns: gently pull off the heads and shells, but leave the tails on, and then use a toothpick to remove the black, thread-like gut.

In a small bowl, whisk together the lemon juice and olive oil to emulsify; season well, then stir in the parsley. Divide the marinade into two bowls, reserving one.

Dip the prawns in one bowl of the marinade, then put them on a plate, cover, and refrigerate for 30 minutes, discarding any remaining marinades.

Remove from the fridge and serve.

Hot buttered crab

This is best made with a freshly picked crab, using both brown and white meat.

Preheat the broiler to hot. Put the crabmeat into a bowl and mix with the nutmeg, olive oil, sherry vinegar, a big dash of Tabasco, and the salt and pepper. Add about three-quarters of the breadcrumbs and all the butter. Mix well.

Spoon the mixture into the cleaned crab shells (or into 2 shallow ovenproof dishes), cover with the remaining breadcrumbs, then place under the broiler for 5 minutes, or until golden and piping hot.

{ SERVES 2}

2¼ pounds boiled crabs,
  picked (yielding about
  ¾ pound white meat and
  1 pound dark meat), and shells
  cleaned
a very fine grating of nutmeg
1 tablespoon olive oil
2 tablespoons sherry vinegar
Tabasco sauce
sea salt and freshly ground
  black pepper
⅔ cup fresh breadcrumbs
4 tablespoons (½ stick) unsalted
  butter, melted

Proper crab cakes

{ SERVES 2 }

½ pound cooked
  white crabmeat
¼ pound cooked
  brown crabmeat
2 teaspoons all-purpose flour
1 egg yolk
½ teaspoon Tabasco sauce
¼ teaspoon Worcestershire
  sauce
pinch of sea salt
large pinch of cayenne pepper
¾ cup fine breadcrumbs
2–3 tablespoons olive oil
1–2 lemons, cut into wedges,
  to serve

I'm fed up with those recipes that demand more potato than crab. Here, you actually get to taste the fat hunks of brown and white meat. Both are essential. You can pick your own meat (it's easy, if time-consuming) or buy it fresh from the fishmonger. Don't bother with the pasteurized stuff for this recipe—the sweetness has long departed.

Mix the crabmeat with the flour, then mix in the egg yolk, Tabasco, Worcestershire sauce, salt, and cayenne.

Put the breadcrumbs in a shallow dish. Shape some of the crab mixture into a plum-size cake, then roll in the breadcrumbs, patting gently to cover. Repeat until you have used all the crab mixture.

Heat the olive oil in a frying pan until very hot, then cook the crab cakes for about 3 minutes on each side, until golden brown. They're fragile and crumbly, so turn carefully. Drain on paper towels and serve with wedges of lemon.

Griddled asparagus with duck egg

As with any asparagus dish, this is only worth doing with English asparagus, in season from the end of April to the start of June. The natural sugars turn to starch within moments of being cut. Get them as fresh as you can, with pert stalks, tight tips, and a base that isn't too woody. Try to buy direct from the source. Even better, pick your own. I once heard of a man so obsessed with eating asparagus fresh that he camped out beside his crown of asparagus the night before he was due to harvest them. As the sun rose the next day, the water was already boiling on a propane stove. At first light, he cut a dozen, simmered them quickly, and ate with a pinch of salt. His verdict: pretty damned good. For the rest of us, a few hours journey from field to fork is fine. The duck eggs ooze their wonderful richness over the green stalks: the perfect partner to this late-spring feast.

{ SERVES 2 }

12 asparagus spears
extra-virgin olive oil
sea salt and freshly ground
   black pepper
2 duck eggs
2 slices of good bread

Heat a griddle pan over a high heat. Brush the asparagus spears with olive oil and season with salt and pepper. Cook on the griddle for 3–4 minutes, until the stems are tender to the tip of a sharp knife. Keep warm.

To poach the duck eggs, use a frying pan with a lid: half-fill with water, bring to the boil, crack in the eggs, cover the pan, remove from the heat, and leave for 3 minutes. Drain on paper towels.

Toast the bread on the griddle pan until it is crisp, with good charred markings. Top each slice of toast with the griddled asparagus and perch a poached duck egg on top.

Jeremy's baked asparagus

{ SERVES 4–5 }

sea salt and freshly ground
  black pepper
20 asparagus spears, woody
  stems trimmed
1 (¼-pound) package (10 sheets)
  feuilles de brick
7 tablespoons (¾ stick plus 1
  tablespoon) unsalted butter,
  melted and kept just warm
1½ ounces Parmesan, finely
  grated
a little olive oil, for greasing

Jeremy Lee is not only one of our finest cooks ("Cook, darling, not chef") but also one of the kindest, funniest, and most intelligent men you'll ever meet. He's now cooking at Quo Vadis in London, and his food is sublime. Of course, this dish only dances onto his menu during spring, made with the freshest British asparagus. But eaten with the fingers, and washed down with blood orange and Campari, it puts a real, *um*, spring into one's step.

If the asparagus is tough-skinned, the pleasure in eating is diminished. Peeling the stalk will set this to rights. *Feuilles de brick* is a Tunisian pastry similar to filo, but cut into large circles.

Preheat the oven to 400°F. Bring a large pot of salted water to a boil and plunge in the asparagus spears. Pop on a lid and bring the water back to a boil. Remove the lid and boil furiously until the asparagus is tender.

Lift the asparagus from the pot, plunge it into iced water, then drain on paper towels before laying it on a tray to cool.

Lay one sheet of pastry on a clean surface, covering the remaining pastry with a damp tea towel to prevent it from drying out. Brush lightly with butter, sprinkle on some of the Parmesan, and season lightly with salt and pepper. Cut the sheet in half and lay a spear of asparagus along the cut edge of each half. Roll the spears tightly in the pastry: you end up with curious-looking sticks, like very long cigarettes. Lay these on a lightly oiled baking sheet and repeat until all the asparagus is wrapped. Put in the fridge for 10 or so minutes to rest.

Put the baking sheets, one or two at a time, in the hot oven and bake for 7–8 minutes, until the pastry is golden brown. Heap on a plate, sprinkle Parmesan all over, and serve swiftly.

Porcini with pappardelle

The porcini, cèpe, or penny bun is not exactly the best-looking of wild mushrooms. With its stout stalk and shiny pate, it's the Mr. Pickwick of the forest floor. It's another particularly generous Antonio Carluccio feast.

Heat the oil and half the butter in a large frying pan until medium hot. Add the mushrooms, salt, and pepper, and increase the heat once the liquid starts to bubble.

Meanwhile, cook the pasta in a large saucepan of salted boiling water. If using fresh, it'll take no more than a couple of minutes. If dried, cook according to the package instructions. Drain.

Add the garlic to the frying pan and cook for a few more minutes, stirring, until the mushrooms take on a tan. Throw in the parsley, then stir into the cooked pasta and serve immediately. Toss with the remaining butter and a drizzle of extra-virgin olive oil.

{ SERVES 4 }

2 tablespoons olive oil, plus extra to serve

3 tablespoons unsalted butter

1 pound fresh porcini, sliced vertically (you can use chanterelles or field mushrooms)

sea salt and freshly ground black pepper

1 pound pappardelle (fresh is best, but dried will do)

2 garlic cloves, finely chopped

handful of flat-leaf parsley, finely chopped

Purple-sprouting broccoli with chillies & anchovies

1 pound purple-sprouting
broccoli (or regular broccoli,
cut into small florets)
2 tablespoons olive oil
2 garlic cloves, finely sliced
1 hottish red chilli (long, thin
one or jalapeño), finely sliced
6 anchovy fillets (those packed
in salt are best, but there are
some decent ones packed in
oil, too), roughly chopped

Preserved anchovies . . . the secret Samaritan. A bit like the Beast or the Hunchback of Notre Dame. Ugly, feared, and misunderstood. But possessing a true heart of gold.

Definitely an acquired taste when eaten raw, once cooked they somehow melt into the background, providing a savoury backbone to any dish. Fish sauce, made from fermented fish, and central to most Southeast Asian cookery, performs a similar role.

Purple-sprouting broccoli is a seasonal treat and one of the few things to emerge from the garden in the lean months of March and April. You can use normal broccoli instead, and that "tender-stem" stuff they sell in the supermarket works beautifully here, too.

Steam the broccoli for 5 minutes.

Heat the oil in a wok or large saucepan over a low heat, and cook the garlic and chilli very gently for about 5 minutes, making sure they don't burn. Add the anchovies, remove from the heat, and bash with a wooden spoon until you have a "fine-ish" mulch.

Return the pan to the heat, add the broccoli, and cook gently for 5–7 minutes more. Serve hot.

Buttered leeks

{ SERVES 4–6 }

10 leeks, roughly chopped into
   rounds, white root ends and
   very extremities of green
   discarded
½ pound plus 2 tablespoons
   (2 sticks plus 2 tablespoons)
   good salted butter, chopped
freshly ground black pepper

Another of the dishes of my youth, this is as easy to make
as it is calorific. Despite a hatred of all those anti-fat finger-
waggers, this certainly verges on the, well, indulgent. You
could put a pat of butter onto a Dan Brown book and it
would taste good. But this is a fine winter dish, and goes
wonderfully with most things.

Preheat the oven to 325°F.

Wash the leeks and allow to dry. Place them in a large
ovenproof dish. Distribute the butter evenly over them,
season with pepper, then bake for 25 minutes until the
leeks are just tender.

{ Salads }

"I cheerfully forget my debtors, but I'll never pardon iceberg lettuce." So wrote the late Ogden Nash, in *Ogden Nash Food* (Stewart, Tabori, and Chang, 1989). And while my sensibilities are not quite as affronted by iceberg lettuce, he does have a point. I love those soft, floppy lettuces, pulled fresh from the garden. They might be less model-like than the iceberg, with its fixed grin and crisp edges. But the flavour is so much better.

A perfect green salad is high art indeed. The dressing must have just the right amount of acidity to cut through the green, but not so much that it puckers the tongue. Each leaf must be washed, then properly dried (buy a salad spinner) so that the dressing sticks. And the amount of dressing is key. Enough to caress, rather than smother the leaves. Four parts good oil to one of vinegar. And a decent whack of either smooth Dijon or English mustard. As to the vinegar, white wine is a good all-purpose choice, while sherry, red wine, and rice vinegars have their own charms.

But there's far more to the salad than mere leaves. Chicken, chorizo, beans, chillies, fennel, and orange are all key players. These aren't salads to pick at, but proper food, for serious eaters.

Chicken liver & chorizo salad

{ SERVES 2 }

1 tablespoon all-purpose flour
salt and freshly ground
 black pepper
6 chicken livers, about
 ½ pound, cleaned and diced
1 tablespoon olive oil
1 small spicy chorizo sausage,
 about ¼ pound, cut into
 ¼-inch-thick slices
2 tablespoons fino sherry
mixed salad leaves, such as baby
 gem lettuce, and watercress
9 ounces cherry tomatoes,
 halved
crusty bread, to serve

For the dressing
¼ cup extra-virgin olive oil
1 tablespoon red wine vinegar,
 or to taste

This is a salad with real punch, contrasting crisp coins of chorizo with tender chunks of chicken liver. Any excess richness is cut through by the sherry and vinegar. A true Iberian feast.

Season the flour with salt and pepper. Coat the chicken livers in the flour, shaking off any excess. Cover and set aside.

Heat the olive oil in a heavy-based frying pan over a medium–high heat and fry the chorizo for 3–4 minutes, or until crisp. Use a slotted spoon to transfer it onto a warm plate, leaving the chorizo-flavoured oil in the pan.

Add the chicken livers to the pan and fry for 2–3 minutes, or until golden brown and just cooked through. Do not overcook. Remove the livers from the pan and add to the chorizo.

Pour off any excess oil from the pan, leaving behind the juices. Return the pan to the heat, pour in the sherry, and stir to deglaze, scraping up any flavoursome brown bits from the bottom of the pan.

To make the dressing, in a small bowl, whisk together the olive oil and vinegar with a pinch of salt and freshly ground black pepper. Taste and add more olive oil or vinegar if necessary. Put the mixed leaves and tomatoes in a bowl and pour enough dressing over to coat lightly; toss gently.

Divide the salad between 2 serving plates, then scatter over the chorizo and chicken livers, pour over the pan juices, and serve with crusty bread.

Romaine & haddock salad

This might seem an incongruous combination on paper but it works beautifully on the plate. The fennel not only adds flavour, but extra texture in contrast to the soft fish and romaine lettuce.

Halve the fennel lengthwise. Cut out the small triangular core, trim the ends, and discard. Slice the remaining fennel as thinly as possible.

Trim the lettuce hearts. Halve lengthwise, halve again, and cut each quarter in half. Rinse and shake dry.

To make the dressing, in a large bowl, whisk together the vinegar, lemon juice, mustard, and olive oil. Season with salt, pepper, and a pinch of sugar.

Toss the fennel and lettuce in the dressing to coat. Season the flour with salt and pepper and dust the fish fillets. Heat the olive oil in a frying pan over a medium–high heat and, when hot, lay in the fillets. Cook for 2–3 minutes on each side, or until the fish is light golden and cooked through.

Divide the salad between 2 plates, top with the fish, and sprinkle with chives.

{ SERVES 2 }

1 small fennel bulb

3 hearts of romaine lettuce

2 tablespoons all-purpose flour

salt and freshly ground
   black pepper

2 (6-ounce) haddock fillets

1 tablespoon olive oil

1 tablespoon chopped chives,
   to serve

For the dressing

½ tablespoon white wine vinegar

squeeze of lemon juice

1 teaspoon smooth
   Dijon mustard

1 tablespoon extra-virgin
   olive oil

pinch of superfine sugar

Smoked eel & bacon salad

{ SERVES 2 }

8 rashers smoked bacon
about 1 pound smoked eel fillet,
  broken into big chunks
1 head of curly endive (frisée),
  separated, washed, and dried
  in a salad spinner

For the dressing
juice of ½ lemon
½ teaspoon smooth English
  mustard
1 teaspoon fresh horseradish
  or ½ teaspoon commercial
salt and freshly ground
  black pepper
3 tablespoons extra-virgin
  olive oil

I love eel. Far from the sinister, flesh-eating beasts of popular imagination, they're actually remarkable creatures, whose life cycle makes the salmon look laid-back. Born somewhere in the vast, strange mass that is the Sargasso Sea, they float over thousands of miles as *leptocephali*— gossamer, leaf-like larvae—at the mercy of predators both above and below, before turning into tiny elvers when they hit brackish water. It's then upstream to find a home and hang about for a few years before fattening up for the journey back home. Epic, in every way.

The British eel fisheries are very well run, but worldwide, stocks are plummeting. Try to buy British and you can eat with conscience clear. The best smoked eel I've ever eaten is from Brown and Forrest in Somerset. Quite incredible. Severn & Wye do a fine product, too. If salad seems too insubstantial, pile it into a good baguette with extra mayonnaise and eat as a sandwich.

To make the dressing, mix the lemon juice with the mustard, horseradish, salt, and pepper. Whisk in the oil to emulsify.

Cook the bacon in a frying pan over a high heat until crisp. Crumble it into big pieces.

Mix the eel and bacon with the endive in a serving bowl, pour the dressing over, and serve.

Green salad

3 hearts of romaine lettuce or
  1 head of floppy lettuce, leaves
  separated, washed, and dried

For the dressing
1 tablespoon white wine vinegar
½ teaspoon smooth French or
  English mustard
sea salt and freshly ground
  black pepper
¼ cup good extra-virgin olive oil

Put the lettuce in a bowl. To make the dressing, mix the vinegar with the mustard, then add a big pinch of salt and a healthy grind of pepper. Whisk in the oil, slowly, so it's properly mixed, or just add and shake in a jam jar.

Carefully dress the salad, a few dribbles at a time, until each leaf is gleaming, not drowning. Finish with a small pinch of salt.

Provençal green bean salad

This reminds me of long, rosé-fuelled lunches at a friend's house in the south of France. You want to cook the beans to just past the squeak point, but not so they're soft and dreary. Use the best olive oil you can find. And do top and tail the beans. Chef Simon Hopkinson is very particular about this and once sent back a plateful of these haricots verts because only the tops were trimmed. He wasn't being fussy, just aesthetically exacting.

Cook the beans in well-salted boiling water for 6 minutes. Drain and refresh in cold water.

Soften the garlic in 1 tablespoon olive oil over a low heat for 3–4 minutes, then add to the beans along with the remaining olive oil, vinegar, and salt and pepper to taste.

{ SERVES 4 }

2¼ pounds green beans (haricots verts), topped and tailed
sea salt and freshly ground black pepper
2 garlic cloves, very finely chopped
2–3 tablespoons extra-virgin olive oil
2 teaspoons white wine vinegar

Oriental cucumber salad

This is one of those dishes that started off rather different to what it is now. I love the crisp, cool flavour of cucumber salad and, mixed with the chicken, chillies, rice wine vinegar, and fish sauce, it suddenly becomes an incredibly healthy dinner. Marinating the meat in *gochujang* (Korean fermented chilli paste), available from Thai supermarkets, adds another layer of flavour. And the two different cuts of the cucumber add an interesting texture. Cool cucumber and hot chicken. Nice.

Put the chicken in a glass bowl and mix with 1 tablespoon of the fish sauce, the juice of 1 lime, and the *gochujang*. Cover and leave to marinate in the fridge for a few hours.

Put all the cucumber in another bowl with 1 tablespoon of fish sauce, the juice of ½ a lime, the rice wine vinegar, and all the chillies. Mix well and check the taste: you may wish to add more fish sauce. Cover and set aside in the fridge for 2 hours.

Add the broccoli, scallions, and shallots to the cucumber, re-cover, and marinate in the fridge for 30 minutes more.

Tip the marinated cucumber mixture into a sieve set over a bowl, reserving any liquid.

Heat the oil in a wok or frying pan over a high heat until smoking. Fry the chicken for 12–15 minutes, turning from time to time, until cooked through and a little crisp at the edges.

In a large bowl, mix the marinated cucumber mixture with the chopped herbs and cooked chicken. Add some of the reserved cucumber marinade, along with the juice of ½ a lime. Taste and check if there's enough fish sauce (there should be a balance of hot, salty, and a little sour) and serve.

Fennel & orange salad

2 largish fennel bulbs
3 oranges
handful of fresh fava beans
  (optional)

For the dressing
juice of ½ orange
juice of ½ lemon
sea salt and freshly ground
  black pepper
3–4 tablespoons extra-virgin
  olive oil

This is a reveille of a salad: fresh and punchy. Fennel and orange make perfect partners. And if you're making this in early summer, a handful of fresh fava beans makes things better still.

Cut the horns off the fennel bulbs, then use a mandoline to slice the bulbs from top to bottom.

Slice off both ends of the oranges, then remove all the peel and pith using a small sharp knife. Carefully cut out the segments.

If using fava beans, dunk them in boiling water, then immediately drain and rinse in cold water and peel.

To make the dressing, mix the orange and lemon juice, season, then whisk in the olive oil (you need twice as much oil as juice).

Divide the fennel, oranges, and beans, if using, between 2 serving plates. Pour the dressing over and serve.

Orange, red onion & basil salad

2 good oranges

1 red onion, sliced into
  thin rings

10 cherry tomatoes, halved

handful of basil, torn

For the dressing

big squeeze of lemon juice

2 tablespoons extra-virgin
  olive oil

sea salt and freshly ground
  black pepper

One of the most refreshing salads I've ever eaten: the orange works in deft harmony with the onion, cutting a wonderfully zingy path through the palate.

Slice off both ends of the oranges. Remove all the peel and pith using a small sharp knife, then cut into horizontal slices. Arrange the orange slices on a plate—nothing too anal, just keep it neatish. Scatter over the onion and tomatoes.

In a small bowl, whisk together the lemon juice and olive oil to emulsify; season well, then drizzle over the onions and tomatoes. Scatter with the basil.

{ Savouries }

Those with a keen interest in affairs of the gut need no introduction to the savoury, that crowning glory of Victorian and Edwardian eating. It arrived in the gap between pudding and fruit. And in the words of Ambrose Heath, who devoted an entire tome, *Good Savouries* (1934), to the matter, they make ". . . an admirable ending to a meal, like some unexpected witticism or amusing epigram at the close of a pleasant conversation. It has the last word, as it were, before we turn to the frivolities of dessert."

Of course, the French were appalled by the very concept. "A savoury, or rather a savoury dish coming at the very end of a dinner," wrote P. Morton Shand in *A Book of Food* (1927), "is regarded by the French as something worse than an anachronism, a deliberate blasphemy against Gastronomea,

Brillat-Savarin's Tenth Muse." No matter, he goes on, for ". . . the course is an essentially English institution. The French loss is our gain." Quite right, too.

These bite-size morsels were usually strong flavoured and toast-based (with the occasional pastry case or soufflé), all possessing those qualities so admired by Mrs. Beeton, the "piquant, rather strong, appetizing flavour essential in a savoury." Cheese played a starring role, along with anchovies, cured pork, and all manner of devilled delights. Welsh rabbit and angels on horseback, soft roes on toast, and curried croútes. As a man whose tastes tend towards the savoury, they represent a release from the tyranny of pudding. If you can't face adding in this extra exquisite course, the following make fine snacks and starters, too.

"Robustly and triumphantly English"

P. Morton Shand, A Book of Food *(Jonathan Cape, 1927)*

Devilled kidneys on toast

{ SERVES 2 }

6 lamb's kidneys, about
  ¾-pound total weight
3 tablespoons all-purpose flour
1 teaspoon cayenne pepper
1 teaspoon English mustard
  powder
sea salt and freshly ground
  black pepper
2 teaspoons unsalted butter
6 tablespoons chicken stock
few drops of Tabasco sauce
1 teaspoon Worcestershire sauce
2 pieces of white toast

In Victorian and Edwardian times, the British were great fans of devilled everything. A pinch of cayenne pepper, some mustard, a splash of anchovy or Worcestershire sauce, and a good knob of butter do wonders to any dish: almonds, biscuits, cutlets, and sardines. Florence White, in *Good Things in England* (1932), mentions a recipe for Boodle's Club Devilled Bones. And very fine they sounded, too. To me the greatest savoury of all is devilled kidneys. This is a proper breakfast dish, but equally civilized for lunch, tea, or dinner. You can use lamb or veal kidneys, but make sure they're fresh, and core them yourself with a pair of scissors.

Snip the white cores out of the kidneys using scissors, rinse with cold water, drain, and pat dry with paper towels.

Mix the flour, cayenne, mustard powder, and salt and pepper together on a plate. Dust the kidneys with the seasoned flour and shake to remove the excess.

Heat a frying pan over a medium–high heat, add the butter and fry the kidneys for 2 minutes each side, or until cooked. Add the stock, Tabasco, and Worcestershire sauce, to taste.

Remove the kidneys from the pan and keep warm. Simmer the sauce for a minute or two until reduced slightly. Serve the kidneys on toast and pour the sauce over.

Crab toasts

You can use pasteurized vacuum-packed crab here, as flavours are bold.

Preheat the broiler to hot. Mix the white and brown crabmeat with the butter, vinegar, lemon juice, mustard, Worcestershire sauce, and Tabasco. Season with salt and cayenne. Taste and adjust as necessary.

Spread the mixture on toast, sprinkle with the grated cheese, then broil for 2 minutes. Sprinkle with the parsley and serve.

{ SERVES 4 }

2 pounds boiled crab, picked
(or use pasteurized crab, about
½ pound white meat and
¼ pound dark meat)
1 tablespoon unsalted butter,
melted, then cooled
1 tablespoon white wine vinegar
juice of ¼ lemon
1 teaspoon smooth English
mustard
½ teaspoon Worcestershire sauce
few drops of Tabasco sauce
pinch of sea salt
pinch of cayenne pepper
4 pieces of brown toast
1¾ ounces good strong
Cheddar, grated
pinch of finely chopped flat-leaf
parsley

English rabbit

{ SERVES 2 }

¼ cup decent English ale
5½ ounces strong Cheddar,
  grated
1 teaspoon Worcestershire sauce
2 teaspoons freshly made
  English mustard
freshly ground black pepper
3 thick slices of good bread

The classic savoury, and basically cheese on toast with a few quid in its back pocket, this is an Anglicized version of Welsh rabbit. Ale, Worcestershire sauce, Cheddar, and English mustard—fine, upstanding ingredients all, stalwarts of the Albion kitchen.

No one can agree as to whether this is "rabbit" or "rarebit". The latter means a delicacy, and could have been corrupted into "rabbit." But "rabbit" appeared in print before rarebit, in Hannah Glasse's *The Art of Cookery Made Plain and Easy* (1747) for a start. Who knows? It tastes equally good, whichever way you spell it.

For the ale, an IPA works well but you don't want anything too heavy, as it tends to overwhelm and bludgeon the cheese into submission. Montgomery's Cheddar is the best in the world (along with Keen's), but if you can't find it, then substitute another strong, decent Cheddar.

Preheat the broiler to hot. Put the ale in a saucepan and bring to a boil to burn off the alcohol and reduce slightly. Take the pan off the heat and stir in the cheese until melted. Add the Worcestershire sauce, mustard, and pepper.

Preheat the broiler to hot. Toast one side of the bread under the grill, turn over, make an indentation, and pour in the cheese. Broil for a minute or two and eat standing up. This is a dish that rarely makes it to the table.

Mushrooms on toast

This is quick-fix comfort food of the finest variety, season of mellow fruitfulness on a plate. Wild mushrooms are best, anything from porcini and chanterelles—all sexy and yellow—to shaggy inkcaps, hedgehog and horse, parasol, and fairy ring. They're free and, if you know where to look, abundant. When setting off on the "silent hunt," ensure you know what you're looking for. *A Passion for Mushrooms* by Antonio Carluccio is comprehensive, as are Roger Phillips's *Wild Food* and Richard Mabey's *Food for Free*. If I'm not sure, I check about four tomes until certain. Death Caps and Destroying Angels live up to their name. And severe liver poisoning, or agonizing death, can prove a real downer on dinner.

{ SERVES 2 }

1 tablespoon olive oil, plus extra for the bread

2 tablespoons unsalted butter

10 ounces wild mushrooms, such as porcini and chanterelles (or even button mushrooms, when wild are out of season)

2 garlic cloves, chopped

squeeze of lemon juice

sea salt and freshly ground black pepper

handful of flat-leaf parsley, roughly chopped

2 big slices of good bread

Heat the oil and butter in a frying pan over a medium heat until foaming. Add the mushrooms and stir, for about 2 minutes, until the juices start to bubble.

Throw in the garlic, lemon juice, salt, and pepper and cook for another few minutes until the mushrooms begin to take on colour. When soft, brown, and a little shrunken, throw in the parsley and mix.

Anoint the bread with olive oil and cook on a griddle pan over a high heat until crisp and golden. Pile the mushrooms on top of the toast. The juices should soak through.

Rhubarb fool

3⅓ pounds rhubarb, cut
  into 1½-inch lengths
1½ cups superfine sugar
juice and grated zest of 1 orange
2⅓ cups heavy cream
7 ounces ginger biscuits or
  cookies, crushed
about ½ cup King's Ginger
  liqueur or Stone's Ginger wine
  (optional)

Great name, and beautifully simple to make. Rhubarb is
my favourite version. Ginger biscuits add wonderful crunch.
Soaking them in King's Ginger liqueur makes it finer still.
As summer goes on, use gooseberries or raspberries instead.

Preheat the oven to 350°F. Put the rhubarb in a casserole
and sprinkle with the sugar, orange juice, and zest. Cover
with a lid and roast for about 40 minutes, until soft. Allow to
cool. Strain the juice and reserve; pick out 18 pieces of
rhubarb for decoration and set aside. Purée the remaining
rhubarb in a food processor.

Whip the cream until it forms soft peaks, not too firm,
then fold in the rhubarb purée along with a few dribbles
of the reserved juice. Don't mix too manically.

Put a layer of crushed biscuits into 6 wine glasses, then
a splash of the ginger booze. Spoon the fool on top and
finish with 3 pieces of rhubarb.

Lemon granita

{ SERVES 4–6 }

2⅛ cups water, filtered if
  possible
1 cup plus 1 tablespoon
  superfine sugar
1 cup fresh lemon juice, about
  6 lemons
vodka (optional)

You'll find granita all over southern Italy and Sicily, served
in bars and sold from the side of the road. The ones made
with lemons from Sorrento are particularly good. The key
is the balance between sharp and sweet. And although this
recipe seems a little hard going (well, not that hard), it is
the best way to ensure you get those perfectly sized pieces
of chipped ice. The technique comes from the wonderful
Ice Creams, Sorbets & Gelati: The Definitive Guide (Grub
Street, 2010) by Caroline and Robin Weir. They've forgotten
more about their subject than I can ever hope to learn.

Bring 1 cup of the water to the boil. Put the sugar
in a bowl and pour over the boiling water. Stir until the
sugar dissolves, then allow to cool. Add the lemon juice
and remaining water to the sugar syrup, stir, and chill in
the fridge for at least 3 hours.

Pour into a strong plastic container, about 19 x 10 x 3 inches:
the mixture should be about ¾ inch deep. Freeze for 1 hour,
until the edges start to ice and the bottom starts to freeze.
Beat hard with fork, scraping every frozen bit away from the
sides and bottom and remixing with the liquid.

Refreeze, then repeat the beating every 30 minutes or so.
Do this four more times, until you have ice crystals that
are loose and smooth. Eat immediately, with a shot of
vodka if you like. (Any leftovers can be stored in the
freezer; beat with a fork once more just before serving.)

Affogato

Simple, but effective. As ever, the quality of ingredients is everything. Nescafé poured over Mr. Whippy just won't cut it. This mixes creamy vanilla ice cream with searing hot, rich, and bitter espresso.

Put a scoop of vanilla ice cream into 2 bowls. Cover with hot coffee. Eat immediately.

{ **SERVES 2** }

2 scoops good vanilla ice cream
2 freshly made single espressos

Hot cider punch

{ SERVES 1 }

3⅔ quarts good dry cider

1 cup plus 1½ tablespoons
  brown sugar

pared rind of 2 oranges

4 whole cloves

2 cinnamon sticks, broken in
  half

2 star anise

big slug of Somerset cider
  brandy or Calvados

I love cider. Not that muck made from concentrate, but the proper, West Country stuff, from the likes of Julian Temperley at Burrow Hill (his Somerset cider brandy is also sublime, especially the Alchemy and 20-Year-Old stuff). I once judged the cider competition at The Royal Bath and West Show. The true pros helped me through over 300 ciders, ranging from liquid silage to apple-based bliss. Spitting out was a necessity. It was still a few weeks before I could face cider again, however good. For more information, buy James Crowden's *Ciderland* (Birlinn, 2008). This is a classic punch, served hot around Halloween, or even Christmas and New Year.

In a large pan, mix the cider and sugar and slowly bring to a boil until the sugar dissolves. Add the orange rind and spices and simmer gently for 15 minutes, then leave to cool. Remove the spices and rind. Bring back to a boil, then serve in cups, adding a slug of Somerset cider brandy to each.

Hot toddy

{ SERVES 1 }

1 teaspoon clear, mild honey

1 fl ounce whisky

1–2 whole cloves

½ cinnamon stick

slice of lemon and juice of
  ½ lemon

This was my mother's sworn recipe to battle every sort of cold and bug. She still swears by it. As children, we made do without the whisky. But it's too good for illness alone, and is the perfect thing to warm up dreary winter's eves.

Mix the honey and whisky in a mug or heatproof glass. Add the cloves, cinnamon, and lemon juice, then top up with just-off-the-boil water and stir. Add a slice of lemon and sip as soon as it doesn't burn your lips.

{ Cocktails }

As every proper person knows, there are only three cocktails worthy of serious consideration: the martini, the negroni, and the bloody Mary. The rest are mere dressing, fleeting fancies and dolled-up nothings, transient concoctions made for those who hate the taste of real booze.

The martini is, of course, the greatest cocktail of them all, so simple yet so fiendishly hard to get right. It's an iconic sip, one that, in the words of Lawrence Durrell, "fairly whistles through the rigging." When I talk about the martini I mean dry, bone-dry, with the vermouth (Martini Extra Dry or Noilly Prat) merely hinted at, rather than sloshed in with a liberal hand. Luis Buñuel, that most fantastic of filmmakers, suggested "simply allowing a ray of sunshine to shine through a bottle of Noilly Prat before it hits the bottle of gin." Winston Churchill thought this a step too far, instead allowing that a mere glance at the vermouth bottle while mixing one's drink is easily ample. Then there's the method of ringing up a friend in Sydney, from London, and putting the receiver next to a bottle of gin. Down in Oz, your mate should do the same with the vermouth. If these methods seem a little too extreme, then a fine mist, spritzed from a small atomizer onto the glass, does the

trick. As does swilling out the glass with vermouth. You want an echo of vermouth, no more.

And a martini is always made from gin. Use vodka, and it's a vodka martini. As there's precious little else in the drink, go for the best. Beefeater, Tanqueray, Sipsmith, or Plymouth are all handsome products and shine on their own. The other key ingredient is ice, lots of it. A lukewarm martini is not just an affront to good taste, but downright obscene, too. The gin or vodka must be kept in the freezer, and the glasses, too. These must be small, containing no more than three or four big sips. Any bigger, and your drink will be warm before it's finished.

As to olive versus twist of lemon, it depends on my mood. Do I want savoury, salty heft, or citrus lift? One variation on the theme is a Gibson, where cocktail sticks heavy with tiny cocktail onions replace the olive or twist.

This is a short, sharp, grown-up drink. But reader beware. As James Thurber so sagaciously noted, "One martini is alright, two are too many, three are not enough." One last thought. Bond was wrong when he asked for shaken. It kills the smoothness, dilutes the drink too much. But then even Bond is no match for this most perfect of drinks.

Dry martini

{ SERVES 1 }

dry French vermouth
4 fl ounces gin (or vodka),
  near-frozen
ice
green olive or twist of
  lemon rind

Put 2 martini glasses in the freezer for a few hours.

Fill a small atomizer with vermouth, then spray a fine mist on the frozen martini glasses—or just wash out the glass with a jig of vermouth and pour away the excess.

Mix the gin (or vodka if you're making a vodka martini) with ice in a shaker or mixing glass, stirring about 50 times before straining into the vermouth-sprayed glass. Add an olive or a twist of lemon rind and serve immediately.

Negroni

{ SERVES 1 }

ice
1 part Martini Rosso
1 part Campari
1 part gin

The second of the great cocktails is the negroni, that ruby-red, super-bitter beauty that seems so civilized, yet packs a mighty punch. It's a drink you grow into. My grandparents adored them, but we children thought them most peculiar. And pretty disgusting, too. But like the martini, they make for a perfect apéritif, clearing the palate and fuzzing the brain in the most civilized of ways.

They also provide endless postprandial entertainment, as I found out last year in Sicily. After a vast dinner of spaghetti with sea urchins, *arancini*, and raw prawns, we made jugs of the stuff and evening turned swiftly into morning. Everyone always seemed to end up in the pool. The hangover, though, is fierce. As with the martini, ice is key, and lots of it. It offers the only respite from this boozy onslaught and, like the martini, there's no fruit juice or soda water to bring relief. Always leave for a couple of minutes after making, to mellow.

Fill 2 tumblers with ice. Add the Martini Rosso, Campari, and gin. Stir, then leave for 2 minutes before drinking.

Bloody Mary

The third in the Triumvirate of great cocktails is the bloody
Mary. This is lunch in a glass, the ultimate restorative, a
mighty *mélange* that soothes and excites in equal measure.
The tomato juice floods down the throat, lifted by the
lemon, while the kick comes from the Tabasco, and depth
from Worcestershire sauce. It's a drink that transcends
class, equally at home in a grotty pub as it is, silver-served,
in some sumptuous stately home. Horseradish has no place
in the drink, needlessly sullying an already perfect party.
Though many would disagree. I like a dash of fino sherry,
too, and best of all, Clamato, that MSG-rich tomato drink
made richer still with clam juice. It's thin and perfect when
poured over crushed ice. Le Caprice, in London, makes the
daddy of them all. Lemon is key, at least a half per shaker,
rather than the wretched, and decidedly token, pub or
aeroplane sliver. Tabasco is to taste, although I see little
point in a timid hand. This is supposed to shock you back
into life. And shake the drink, too, with lots of ice, hard for
30 seconds. Then pour and take that first sip. The pupils
dilate, the heart beats faster, and last night's excess begins
to clear from your brain. This is love in a glass. Bloody
Mary, I bow down at your scarlet knees.

{ SERVES 1 }

ice
a very generous slug of vodka
a good glug of Tabasco sauce
juice of ½ lemon
a few glugs of
   Worcestershire sauce
a snifter of fino sherry
a grinding of black pepper
tomato juice, or Clamato if you
   can find it, enough to fill a
   shaker three-quarters full

Put plenty of ice in a shaker. Add the vodka, followed
by Tabasco, lemon juice, and Worcestershire sauce, then
sherry, pepper, and tomato juice. Shake hard as hell for
30 seconds, then serve, ice cold.

{ Slow & low }

Imagine a life of sybaritic indolence, where work is a dirty word and physical exercise, save in matters amatory, an aberration. Transport between bedroom and dining room, the two centers of your universe, is via sedan chair, carried by a sextet of Nubian dancing girls. Grapes are peeled and dropped into your mouth by blushing virgins. And an entire army of eunuchs is employed solely to squeeze lemon on to your breakfast oysters. Fun for a day or two, sure, but tiring after a while. And rather dull, too. Your flesh might be soft, tender, and perfumed, but your character could be somewhat lacking.

It's the same with the more expensive cuts of meat. The chicken breast might offer snowy-white expanses of succulent flesh, but in terms of flavour, it's an also-ran compared to the thighs, wings, or legs. Beef fillet and tenderloin have exceptionally idle lives, sitting pretty under the backbone and barely lifting a finger. So it's beautifully tender, but can fall short in terms of taste. That's not to say there's no place for a good filet steak or plump chicken breast. Far from it. But if it's pure meaty heft you're after, then you want the cuts of meat that have done some work.

These cuts, from cheek to tail, shin to shank, are often cheaper, but tougher, too. They demand low, slow cooking, so all that connective tissue is broken down, transforming inedible collagen into soft, melting gelatin. You'll end up with great chunks of meat soft enough to cut with a spoon. This is culinary alchemy at its very finest.

This is a chapter devoted to low, slow cooking. The sort of dish that might require a little work at the start but is then left to blip and bubble away for hours. Some sit atop the stove in a barely simmering swell, others dwell in ovens no warmer than a tropical breeze.

A couple require no direct heat at all, rather the constant flow of the sweetest smoke. From proper ribs to oxtail stew, these dishes take time. But there's something deeply satisfying about taking a tough old piece of meat, lavishing it with love and low heat, and seeing it fall apart into silken strands. On the whole, these are one-pot dishes, and I can't get too excited about the differences between stew and daube, braise and casserole. To the pedant and purist, there are many, but none so important as to trouble us here. It's merely a question of kitchen semantics.

Browning of meat

Some recipes require the meat to be browned first. This does not (and never has) seal in the moisture, whatever a thousand witless TV chefs might profess. Harold McGee, author of *On Food and Cooking* (Hodder & Stoughton, 1984), has long proved this errant. No, one browns meat to get more flavour, thanks to the wonders of the Maillard reaction. Named after Louis Camille Maillard, a French physician and chemist, this is the process that creates the cooked colour and flavour of everything, from bread crust and roasted coffee to dark beers and roasted meats. On meat, it produces that wonderful caramelized crust. But you do need a high heat. Heat the oil until it smokes, then brown the meat in batches (if you overfill the pan, the meat will sweat rather than brown. Like me sitting by the pool). Drop it in, leave for about a minute, then turn and leave for the same amount of time. You want dark-brown streaks rather than insipid gray hues.

Tom's 10-alarm chili

{ **SERVES 10** }

2–4 tablespoons peanut oil

8 pounds shin of beef, chopped
  into about 10 big chunks

4 red onions, finely chopped

6 dried chipotle chillies, soaked
  in water for 30 minutes,
  then finely chopped

6 dried ancho chillies, soaked in
  water for 30 minutes,
  then finely chopped

4 habanero chillies,
  finely chopped

5 garlic cloves, finely chopped

3 tablespoons cumin seeds,
  roasted in a hot dry pan until
  the oils are released, then
  ground to a fine powder

2 big pinches of Mexican
  oregano (or use European
  oregano if you must)

½ teaspoon cayenne pepper

½ teaspoon hot chili powder

4 tablespoons tomato purée

Tabasco sauce

Worcestershire sauce

1 quart fresh beef stock (a
  decent cube will do)

grated Cheddar cheese, sour
  cream, crushed crackers,
  chopped red onion, fresh
  cilantro leaves, and tortillas or
  boiled white rice, to serve

Chili. One word, one million different ways with meat and spice. Forget those insipid, second-rate British versions, which are little more than mince with a sombrero, and delusions of greatness. In the southwestern United States, chili (note the single "l") is less dish and more cult, art, and religion all rolled into one. The perfect "bowl of red," as it's affectionately known, is a very serious subject, with endless books devoted to its creation, and cook-offs raging non-stop. In Texas, it's a capital offence to add beans; in New Mexico, they like it pure; just meat and purée mixed together, no vegetables.

"When speaking of a bowl of red, I refer to chili con carne," wrote the late chili maestro Frank X. Tolbert in his seminal *A Bowl of Red*, "honest-to-God chili, and not the dreadful stuff masquerading as chili that is served in nine out of ten cafés." Texas chili is my favourite, chunks of beef (or coarse ground if you must) slow-cooked with onions, garlic, Mexican oregano, freshly ground cumin seeds, and chillies, fresh and dried. And remember, no beans.

Although chili sounds Mexican, and often tastes it, too, this is most certainly American. Some claim it's descended from a dish eaten by Texas pioneers on the road to California gold fields. Dried beef, chillies, suet, and salt would be pounded together into a rather stodgy brick. Once on the trail, strips could be ripped off and boiled up to provide a decent dinner. Others argue that chili was a cowboy dish, using a surfeit of beef jazzed up with wild chillies picked on the open plains.

Whatever the truth, it's a poor man's dish at heart, but one best cooked in big vats. There are few finer sights than a great pot of the stuff, bubbling atop the stove. My friend James used to have a chili cook-off at his house in the week before Christmas. He favours a tomato-based, minced meat version with beans. It is pretty damned good, though, and his recipe follows mine. Just don't make it in Texas.

{ **CONTINUES OVERLEAF** }

The key here is the cumin and mix of fresh, dried, and powdered chillies. You want spice, warmth, and richness. Serve with tortillas, or a huge mound of plain white rice. Grated cheese and saltine crackers are traditional, too, and a big bowl of sour cream.

"Chili eaters is some of Your chosen people," goes a famous chili prayer. "We don't know why You so doggone good to us. But, Lord God, don't never think we ain't grateful for this chili we about to eat. Amen."

⌣

Preheat the oven to 275°F.

Heat 2 tablespoons peanut oil in a very large enamelled casserole over a high heat and brown the meat, in batches, then set aside.

In the same pot, add a little more oil and soften the onions over low to medium heat for about 10 minutes, then add all the chopped chillies and garlic and cook gently for 5 minutes. Open the windows, as the fumes released are pretty eye-watering. Add more oil as you go if needed.

Add the cumin, oregano, cayenne, and chili powder and cook for a minute or so more. Then add the tomato purée and a big glug each of Tabasco and Worcestershire sauce and cook for 2 minutes more.

Return the browned meat to the pot, stir, then add the stock. Bring just to the boil, then cover and cook in the oven for 4–5 hours until the meat is meltingly tender. Serve with grated cheese, sour cream, crushed crackers, chopped red onion, fresh cilantro leaves, and either tortillas or boiled rice.

James's "Old Bank" chili

"It's the mix of lamb and beef as well as the Moroccan harissa paste that gives this chili its taste," says my friend James. He gets his harissa paste from the market in Marrakech and stores it in olive oil. If Morocco is too far, then most supermarkets have a decent alternative. "This is one of the key ingredients and gives a great flavour without going overboard on the heat. And leaving the chili overnight, once cooked, allows the magic to happen." The only thing I'd disagree with is his advice about serving it with brown rice. In my view, this is best left to the hippies. But it's his recipe, and damned fine it is, too. You can freeze any you don't eat.

Heat 2 tablespoons olive oil in a frying pan, add the chillies, onions, garlic, and peppers and cook until soft.

Heat the remaining olive oil in a very large enamelled casserole over a high heat and brown all the meat, in batches. Add more oil as you go if needed. Return all the meat to the pot. Add the chilli and onion mixture, then add half the wine and all the canned tomatoes, passata, harissa paste, and Worcestershire sauce. Turn the heat right down and simmer, uncovered, stirring occasionally, for 1 hour.

Add the kidney beans and the rest of the wine and leave to simmer for another hour, or until the chili is the required consistency. If it is too dry, add more passata and red wine (you can never have enough). If too wet, keep simmering. Taste for salt and heat and adjust accordingly, adding a little more harissa paste if you like.

Leave the chili to sit overnight, covered, in the fridge: this lets the flavours meld together into something amazing. The next day, reheat the chili until heated through and serve with sour cream, grated Cheddar, and boiled brown rice.

{ SERVES 10 }

4 tablespoons olive oil
5–10 bird's-eye chillies, finely chopped
3 big white onions, finely chopped
cloves from 1 head of garlic, finely chopped
3 red bell peppers, seeded and finely chopped
2¼ pounds ground beef
2¼ pounds ground lamb
1 (75 cl) bottle of punchy red wine
3 (14.5-ounce) cans chopped tomatoes
6 cups tomato passata
2 tablespoons harissa chilli paste, or more, to taste
3 tablespoons Worcestershire sauce
3 (15-ounce) cans red kidney beans, drained and rinsed
sea salt
sour cream, grated Cheddar, and boiled brown rice to serve

Pot-au-feu

2 pounds shin of beef, in one
 piece
2 pounds silverside of beef
 (or topside)
1⅓ pounds oxtail, cut into thick
 pieces
6 carrots, roughly chopped
4 leeks, white and light-green
 parts only, roughly chopped
2 celery stalks, roughly chopped
3 large onions, halved, one half
 studded with 3 whole cloves
1 head of garlic, left whole
2 tomatoes, halved
6 whole peppercorns
1 bouquet garni (2 bay leaves,
 1 sprig of celery leaves, 3 sprigs
 of thyme, 4 parsley leaves,
 stalks, and, if possible, roots,
 too, all tied together in a piece
 of cheesecloth)
2 beef marrowbones (optional)
 (get the butcher to saw them in
 half or quarter them,
 depending on the size of
 your pan)
sea salt and freshly ground
 black pepper

If ever three words were imbued with Gallic history, pride, and delight, they are *pot-au-feu*. For this is no mere stew, rather a cornerstone of French cuisine, a dish that spans regions and classes like some meat-scented Colossus. "In France," wrote no lesser an authority than Auguste Escoffier, "the *pot-au-feu* is the symbol of family life . . . A good *pot-au-feu* will always be a comfortable and thoroughly bourgeois dish that nothing may dethrone." Revolutionary, writer, and all-around Renaissance man, the Comte de Mirabeau went one step further. "The foundation of empires," he proclaimed proudly.

Pot-au-feu's origins lie in the ever-simmering soup pot, traditionally found at the back of most French kitchens, into which bones, vegetables, and scraps of meat would be thrown. It would be continually eaten and replenished. And if the family had money, pieces of meat would be added.

There are myriad versions of *pot-au-feu* in France, each region united in the certainty that its version is the only one of any merit. As the name suggests, though, this is just a pot over the fire and open to all manner of interpretation. In the Languedoc, there's beef, bacon, and cabbage. Up near the Pyrenees, by Tarn, a stuffed bird is added. (Some favour stuffed goose neck, others raw ham, salt pork, confit duck, mutton, goose, and cabbage). The key is mixing different flavours and textures: gelatinous, fatty, and lean. The broth is drunk first, and the meat served with mustard, pickles, horseradish, and pickled onions. You will need a very big pot, for this is a feast, best served to a big table of ravenous guests.

Place both pieces of beef and the oxtail in a large enamelled casserole, or stainless-steel pot or stockpot and cover with cold water. Bring slowly to a boil, then simmer until scum forms and skim off the scum. Continue simmering and repeating the skimming for 10 minutes, until the scum changes from mucky gray to white froth. Tip away the water, return the beef and oxtail to the pan, and cover with fresh cold water.

Add the carrots, leeks, celery, onions, garlic, tomatoes, peppercorns, and bouquet garni and bring to the boil. Turn down to the merest simmer, cover with a lid (leaving a small gap), and simmer gently for 2 hours. Add the marrowbones and simmer gently for a further 1–1½ hours.

Allow to cool, then skim off any excess fat. Strain the broth into a clean pan and bring back to a boil. Season to taste. Pour over slices of baguette in bowls and top with a sprinkling of grated Gruyère. Scoop out the cooked marrow and add to the bouillon along with the soft garlic cloves, discarding the papery skins.

Serve the meat and vegetables with a pile of good salt, the mustards, cornichons, pickled onions, and horseradish.

To serve
1 baguette, sliced
6–7 ounces Gruyère, grated
a small bowl of sea salt
Dijon mustard
English mustard
cornichons
small pickled onions
freshly grated horseradish

Boeuf en daube

I remember this dish from Virginia Woolf's *To the Lighthouse*. Actually, it's about all I remember from the book, the ". . . . exquisite scent of olive and oil and juice" rising from the dish as the top was taken off. It took Mrs. Ramsay's maid, Mildred, three days to cook, although this seems a touch excessive. Overnight in the marinade, I suppose, then a few hours in a low oven. It's always better the next day anyway. But the ever-anxious hostess's frets about it being spoiled, thanks to the guests coming in late, are unfounded. This daube improves as it's heated and cooled down, and is also wonderful cold. Cooked properly, this is robust enough to deal with all manner of tardy diners.

Put the beef in a nonreactive dish and cover with the marinade ingredients. Cover with plastic wrap and refrigerate overnight. When you are ready to cook the daube, preheat the oven to 275°F. Lift the beef out of the marinade and drain. Strain the marinade into a container and reserve. Heat the oil in a large heavy-bottomed enamelled casserole over a high heat and brown the meat on both sides. Remove and set aside.

In the same casserole, cook the bacon and pork rinds, if using, over a medium–high heat until crisp; remove and set aside. Lay half the bacon and rinds in the casserole. Add the carrots, onions, parsley, bay leaf, garlic, orange rind, and remaining bacon. Put the beef on top and pour over the reserved marinade and red wine to cover, followed by the remaining rinds and the tomatoes. Bring to a boil, cover with foil and a tight lid, and bake for 2½–3 hours until tender.

If you can, leave to cool, skim off the fat, remove the parsley stalks and bay leaves, and leave in the fridge, covered, overnight. Reheat thoroughly the next day, adding the black olives. If the sauce seems thin, lift out the meat and vegetables with a slotted spoon and keep warm while you boil the sauce for 5–10 minutes to thicken. Serve the daube with cooked noodles doused in olive oil, or plain rice.

{ SERVES 6 }

3 pounds top rump of beef or shin, cut into "squares," in the words of Elizabeth David, "the size of half a postcard" and about ½ inch thick

2 tablespoons olive oil

5 rashers unsmoked streaky bacon, cut into small pieces

3 ounces fresh pork rinds (optional)

3 carrots, cut into ½-inch slices

3 onions, finely chopped

4 parsley stalks

1 bay leaf

2 garlic cloves, bruised

small strip of pared orange rind

½ (75-cl) bottle of good red wine

4 tomatoes, peeled, seeded, and sliced

handful of good black olives, pitted

cooked noodles or white rice, to serve

For the marinade

½ (75-cl) bottle of good red wine

2 tablespoons olive oil

a few sprigs of thyme

4 garlic cloves, bruised

1–2 sprigs of rosemary

2 bay leaves

5 black peppercorns, crushed

Boeuf Bourguignon

4 tablespoons olive oil

1 small onion, roughly chopped

8 garlic cloves, bruised with
back of knife

1 large carrot, roughly chopped

2 celery stalks, roughly chopped

4 sprigs of thyme

2 bay leaves

1 (75-cl) bottle of decent red
Burgundy

1 cup beef stock (best you can
find, although cubes are just
about OK)

4 tablespoons (½ stick) unsalted
butter

¼ pound smoked lardons or
smoked streaky bacon,
chopped into small pieces

5½ ounces button mushrooms

24 button/pearl onions, peeled
(plunge into boiling water for
a minute first), or 14 ounces
small shallots

sea salt and freshly ground
black pepper

2 tablespoons all-purpose flour

2¼ pounds topside of beef,
fat left on and cut into largish
chunks, the size of a small
lady's fist

There's no point beating around the bush. Making this
rich, wonderful Burgundian classic takes time. And the
ingredients look daunting. There are mushrooms, lardons,
pearl onions, and beef, all needing to be browned. There
are sauces to reduce and strain, trotters to be hewn in half,
fat to be skimmed. But none of it actually requires masses
of skill. It takes a good few hours to prepare, and is best
eaten the next day.

I once cooked it for thirty people, and the house stank of
browned everything for days afterwards. But if you enjoy
cooking, you'll love this. Arm yourself with a glass of wine,
turn on some Allman Brothers, and spend an afternoon
soaked in good Burgundy.

As to ingredients, I like topside as it has a good amount
of fat and suits slow cooking. You could use shin, too.
And track down the tiny pearl onions. Any greengrocer
worth his, well, onions, will have them. The pig's trotter
is optional, but your butcher should give you one for free—
get him or her to split it, and if you're worried about it
fitting it into your pot, ask for it to be cut in half crosswise.
The trotter adds a wonderful gelatinous wobble to the dish.

Heat 2 tablespoons of the oil in a frying pan, add the onion,
and soften over a medium heat for 5 minutes. Add the
garlic, carrot, and celery and slightly caramelize, without
burning.

Add the thyme and bay leaves, then pour in the wine.
Bring to the boil and ignite the wine (stand well back and
watch it like a hawk; pull it off the heat if you feel it burns

for too long). Once the flame has gone, add the stock and turn down the heat. Simmer for 30 minutes, or until reduced by half. Strain the liquid into a large container and set aside. Discard the vegetables.

Preheat the oven to 275°F. Melt the butter and remaining olive oil in a large heavy-bottomed enamelled casserole over a medium–high heat. Fry the lardons or bacon until crisp, then set aside. Brown the mushrooms in the same pot, then remove, add more oil, if necessary, and brown the pearl onions. Scrape the bottom of the pot occasionally to remove any crusty bits.

Season the flour. Roll the beef in the flour and brown in batches in more oil, if necessary; set aside. Do the same with the pig's trotter until burnished. Leave the trotter in the pot, pour out any excess fat, and return the bacon, mushrooms, pearl onions, and beef to the pan. Turn up the heat and deglaze the pot with the Cognac. Ignite, let it burn out, then pour in the sauce you made earlier. Bring to a simmer and skim.

Cover with a lid and put the casserole in the oven for 3–3½ hours, or until the beef is tender.

Remove and discard the trotter. Check the seasoning and leave to cool. Remove any fat from the top of the casserole. If possible, leave in the fridge overnight to ensure a polite exchange of flavours. Reheat thoroughly, add the lemon juice and parsley, stir in the Dijon mustard, and serve with mashed potatoes.

1 pig's trotter, split lengthwise (optional)
⅓ cup Cognac
juice of ½ lemon
1 tablespoon flat-leaf parsley, finely chopped
1 tablespoon Dijon mustard

Home-made salt beef

6 pounds rolled brisket

2 carrots, roughly chopped

2 onions, roughly chopped

1 celery stalk, roughly chopped

4 garlic cloves

1 bouquet garni (2 bay leaves,
  1 sprig of celery leaves, 3 sprigs
  of thyme, 4 parsley leaves,
  stalks, and, if possible, roots,
  too; all tied together in a piece
  of cheesecloth)

boiled potatoes, to serve

freshly grated horseradish, to
  serve

For the brine

1½ pounds rock salt

1½ cups demerara sugar

1 dried habanero chilli
  (optional)

3 small dried chillies

3 bay leaves

10 whole black peppercorns

2 star anise

2 whole cloves

2 sprigs of thyme

5 garlic cloves

1 ounce Prague Powder No. 1
  (this is the saltpeter,
  and optional)

This is an epic recipe, but it's more *Independence Day* than *Odyssey* as the action takes place over about eight or so days. Home-made salt beef is miles removed from the bland, chewy, pre-sliced stuff you get in the shops. It's rich and luscious, scented with spices, and falls apart in great chunks.

As to its history, there are the usual debates, arguments, and polite exchanges of opinion. A recipe for pickled beef, in Robert May's *The Accomplisht Cook*, was published in 1660. And the Irish were responsible for creating the lucrative export market right up until the nineteenth century, when British-canned South American beef (far cheaper) took over.

Wherever there was beef, there would have been a preserved version. In the days before refrigeration, the salting of meat was essential. But for me, salt beef is associated with the food of the Ashkenazi Jews of Central and Eastern Europe. Thanks in part to *kashruth*, the strict Jewish dietary laws, only the tough forequarters, away from the rump, could be used. And they had to be cooked within 72 hours of slaughter. Without time to hang and tenderize, salting and slow cooking was the best way to turn tough meat into stuff that could be eaten with a spoon. The East and West End of London, along with most of New York, used to be packed with salt-beef bars. Now, only a few remain, the best of which in London is the Brass Rail at Selfridges.

To get the proper pink tinge, saltpeter is essential. But if you can't get hold of it, worry not, as the flavour remains the same. Either eat it hot, carved into thick slices, with horseradish and boiled potatoes, or cold, sliced very thinly, on rye bread, slathered with English mustard.

As to the pickling receptacle, a big strong bag is most practical. Try Lakeland (www.lakeland.co.uk), the Mecca

for all kitchen supplies. I've also used a washing-up bowl.
Make sure it fits in the fridge and the liquid completely
covers the meat.

To make the brine, put all the ingredients into a large pot
with a gallon water, bring to a boil, then simmer for 4
minutes. Turn off the heat and allow to cool completely.

Put the beef into a nonmetallic bowl (or strong, clean plastic
bag or washing-up bowl), cover with brine (using a plate to
weight down if necessary), and cover with plastic wrap.
Leave in the fridge for about 7 days, turning every day.

Rinse the beef and soak overnight in fresh water.

Discard the soaking water and put the beef into a pot with
the carrots, onions, celery, garlic, and bouquet garni. Cover
with fresh water, bring to a boil, and simmer gently,
covered, for 2–2½ hours, or until very tender. Remove the
bouquet garni and discard along with the liquid and veg.
Serve hot, with boiled potatoes and horseradish, or cold,
with mustard.

Carbonade flamande

{ SERVES 6 }

2–2½ tablespoons beef dripping

4 onions, thinly sliced

3 tablespoons all-purpose flour

2 teaspoons English
  mustard powder

salt and freshly ground black
  pepper

2¼ pounds stewing steak, cut
  into 1½-inch cubes

2 tablespoons red wine vinegar

1½ cups Belgian blond beer

½ cup beef stock

1 tablespoon brown sugar

1 bouquet garni (2 bay leaves,
  1 sprig of celery leaves, 3 sprigs
  of thyme, 4 parsley leaves,
  stalks, and, if possible, roots,
  too; all tied together in a piece
  of cheesecloth)

1 tablespoon Dijon mustard

mashed potatoes, to serve

I wouldn't want to be a Belgian. Tintin was always inferior to Asterix, and Poirot dreamt up by an English Dame. OK, so Jean-Claude Van Damme is a kick-ass legend. And they're good with mussels, chips, and beers. And feeding those great bloated Eurocrats who infect the EU. But please don't bang on about their chocolates. They all taste the same—overbearing and smugly rich. Still, their beer's alright. Choose a decent one for this dish, something with a bite of bitter. A good Abbey Blond beer will work.

As to the name, it's actually Spanish in origin and means "grilled over coals." Whereas this is a slow-cooked stew. Belgians, eh? Still, it's a cracking good stew.

Preheat the oven to 300°F. Heat 1 tablespoon of the dripping in a heavy-based frying pan and fry the onions until lightly coloured but not brown. Lift out with a slotted spoon and transfer to a shallow lidded casserole.

In a shallow bowl, combine the flour with the mustard powder, salt, and pepper and toss the meat in this to coat.

Heat the remaining dripping in the frying pan over a high heat. Brown the meat in batches and transfer to the casserole.

Add the vinegar, beer, and stock to the frying pan with the sugar and bouquet garni. Season to taste and stir until simmering, scraping any residue from the bottom of the pan.

Pour the sauce over the meat and onions, cover tightly, and cook in the oven for 3 hours, or until very tender.

Remove the bouquet garni and stir in the Dijon mustard. Serve with mashed potatoes.

Ragù alla Bolognese

The standard British spaghetti Bolognese is a relentlessly gloomy affair. Take one over-the-hill onion, and maul, before dumping into searing vegetable oil and cooking until the edges are burnt and bitter and the center resolutely hard. Do the same to a couple of cloves of garlic, then throw in a package or two of economy mince, all gray and gristly. And overcook. Remember to overload the pan, so the meat boils rather than browns. Only then will you turn the beef into the rubbery, bovine pellets that are so essential to this hateful dish. Seasonings come next, a splodge of ketchup, an overdiluted stock cube, and a dusty handful of impotent dried herbs. Boil indiscriminately for 20 minutes, then mix with a glut of overcooked, claggy pasta. Finish with a dusting of vomit-scented "Parmesan-style" powder and serve with a grimace. An insipid car crash of a creation, this is food as lowest common denominator, little more than barely edible depression.

Of course, spaghetti Bolognese is one of those Frankenstein's monster sort of beasts, where a great European regional dish (in this case, the *ragù alla Bolognese*) sets off abroad and returns almost unrecognizable with new accent, name, and nose job. "When the Italians emigrated to the United States, just before the Great War, they'd bring with them foods that would last the journey, long bundles of spaghetti and the like," says the Queen of Italian gastronomy, Anna del Conte. "And when they arrived, they added meat to the classic tomato sauce. So spaghetti Bolognese was born, and the American invention eventually made it over to England, and London's Soho in particular." It became so popular that it even returned to parts of Italy.

{ CONTINUES OVERLEAF }

{ SERVES 6 }

2 tablespoons (¼ stick) unsalted butter
2 tablespoons olive oil
1 onion, finely chopped
1 carrot, finely chopped
1 celery stalk, finely chopped
2 garlic cloves, finely chopped
1 bouquet garni (2 bay leaves, 1 sprig of celery leaves, 3 sprigs of thyme, 4 parsley leaves, stalks, and, if possible, roots, too; all tied together in a piece of cheesecloth)
¼ pound chicken livers, rinsed, trimmed, and finely chopped
¼ pound pancetta or unsmoked bacon, finely chopped
¾ pound ground beef, pork, or veal, or a mixture
1¼ cups red wine
sea salt and freshly ground black pepper
4 tablespoons tomato purée
1¼ cups fresh beef stock
2⁄3-cup heavy cream
tagliatelle, to serve
freshly grated Parmesan, to serve

The most elegant and perceptive of women, I'm surprised Anna can still look me in the eye, after an incident where I managed to soak her exquisite cashmere twin set in greasy muck. She was sitting at a table with my co-presenter Matthew Fort, during a recording of *Market Kitchen* for what was then UKTV Food. While I was gurning at the camera, I heard Matthew say something particularly irritating (probably some nonsense about not seasoning your steak before cooking, or how rusk in a sausage is an aberration). So I grabbed the nearest projectile, a vast red chilli, and, not actually looking at my target, hurled it with all my might. My aim, alas, was far from true and the pungent pod flew hard into a plate of caponata. I looked up to see Anna dripping in oil and vinegar. She was not amused.

But back to the real *ragù*. Over in Bologna, that great and meaty Italian city, the *ragù* would be served with fresh tagliatelle, those thickish ribbons a perfect partner to the rich, slow-cooked meat sauce. But pappardelle, penne rigate, and farfalle are all well suited, too, allowing the sauce to stick and nestle in every nook and groove.

And the sauce itself? Well, as ever in matters of European gastronomy, it depends upon whom you ask. Some swear by the addition of tomatoes, while others denounce their inclusion as grotesque. One family might include a good splash of milk or cream for extra smoothness. Another would curse the very thought. Beef and veal are standard, but recipes also include chicken livers, Parma ham, fresh pork, lardo, even game. This is a rich, hefty, slow-cooked sauce, and not only will each region have its own version, but each street and house. Needless to say, the "best" recipe is always their own. Most recipes start with finely chopped celery, carrots, and onions, but not all. The key is the slow, low cook, which transforms tough cuts into silken strands of unctuous delight.

Over the years, I've trawled through many a recipe, and tried them all. Chicken liver, finely chopped, adds not only luscious texture, but real depth of flavour, too. Milk or cream provides lactic bite, and pancetta or prosciutto crudo still more layers of taste. This makes a blissfully rich *ragù*. And one to banish all thoughts of the horrific spag Bol to the culinary rubbish dump for ever.

Heat the butter and oil in a deep saucepan over a medium heat. Add the vegetables, garlic, and bouquet garni and fry until they soften and brown lightly. Add the livers and cook until pink, about 2 minutes. Add the pancetta and minced meat and fry until the meat colours. Add the wine, simmer until it evaporates, then add seasoning, the tomato purée, and a little of the stock. Cook slowly, covered, stirring occasionally and gradually adding more stock.

After 1½ hours, stir in the cream and continue to cook, uncovered, until reduced, about another hour.

Remove the bouquet garni. Cook the tagliatelle and serve with the Bolognese and lots of freshly grated Parmesan.

Oxtail stew

{ SERVES 4 }

2¾ pound oxtail, cut into
   rounds, excess fat removed
sea salt and freshly ground
   black pepper
1 teaspoon cayenne powder
1 teaspoon English
   mustard powder
2 tablespoons all-purpose flour
2 tablespoons olive oil
5 tablespoons (½ stick plus
   1 tablespoon) unsalted butter
2 carrots, roughly chopped
2 onions, roughly chopped
8 closed-cap mushrooms,
   roughly chopped
4 garlic cloves, thinly sliced
4 sprigs of thyme
4 bay leaves
1 (75-cl) bottle of punchy red
   wine such as Rioja or
   Châteauneuf-du-Pape
1 tablespoon Worcestershire
   sauce
1 tablespoon Dijon mustard
handful of flat-leaf parsley,
   roughly chopped

Some of the sweetest meat comes from the cow's tail; wobbling, slightly gelatinous chunks that are the very essence of proper winter food. This is the hale and hearty made flesh. As with so many once-cheap ingredients (pork belly, lamb shanks, pig's cheek), they become trendy, get a taste for Balenciaga and the price rockets. Still, this is a rich, serious dish, spiked with a touch of chilli and mustard, that's best served slopped all over buttery mashed potatoes. Once cooked, leave it in the fridge, covered, overnight. Then reheat the next day.

Soak the oxtail in salted water, covered in the fridge, for a couple of hours. Drain, put into a pan of fresh, unsalted water, and bring to a boil. Reduce the heat and simmer for 15 minutes, then remove from the heat and leave to cool. Pat dry. Preheat the oven to 300°F.

Mix the cayenne and mustard powders in a plastic zip-seal bag with the flour, salt, and pepper. Drop in the oxtail and shake until covered. In a large enamelled casserole, heat the oil and butter over a high heat until foaming, then brown the oxtail in batches. Remove the oxtail and set aside. Reduce the heat slightly and brown the carrots, onions, and mushrooms. When they are browned, add the garlic, thyme, and bay.

Put the oxtail back in the casserole. Add the wine and Worcestershire sauce, season, then bring to a boil and skim off any fat. Cover the casserole and put it into the oven for 3 hours, or until the meat is very tender.

Lift the oxtail onto a plate, pull the meat off the bones, and add back to the stew. Leave overnight in the fridge, covered. The next day, remove the layer of fat from the top of the casserole. Reheat thoroughly until piping hot, stir in the mustard and parsley, and serve with mashed potatoes.

Braised ox cheeks

Like oxtail, ox cheek was once a cheap, dowdy, resolutely
unglamorous cut, but has ascended to the A-list. And I
can see why. Cooked slowly, these cheeks, with all that
hard-working connective fiber, break down into the most
luscious strands. They have a sublime richness and should
be eaten with a spoon, from a bowl.

Season the flour. Chop each ox cheek into 4–6 pieces,
then dust them with the seasoned flour. Heat the oil in a
frying pan over a high heat and brown the meat in batches.
Transfer the meat to a large saucepan or flameproof
casserole. Deglaze the frying pan with a splash of the
beer and pour it over the meat.

Add the celery, leek, and carrots to the casserole and cover
with the stock. Pour in the Worcestershire sauce and the
rest of the beer. Bring to a boil, then reduce the heat
and simmer gently for about 1½ hours, or until the meat
is tender and falling apart.

Remove the meat from the casserole and set aside. Boil
the liquid, uncovered, until it has thickened slightly; about
20 minutes. Return the ox cheeks to the gravy to heat them
through, then serve in a bowl with mashed potatoes and
the gravy.

{ SERVES 4 }

2 tablespoons all-purpose flour
sea salt and freshly ground
    black pepper
2 ox cheeks, about 10½–14
    ounces each (ask your butcher
    to remove the skin and fat)
1 tablespoon vegetable oil
scant 1 cup stout or
    London porter
2 celery stalks, cut into chunky
    matchstick lengths
1 leek, halved and sliced
2 carrots, roughly chopped
1 quart chicken stock
1 tablespoon Worcestershire
    sauce
mashed potatoes, to serve

Oxtail consommé (& Bullshot)

{ SERVES 4–6 }

1 oxtail, about 1⅓ pounds, cut
    into 4 pieces, excess fat
    removed
2 onions, halved lengthwise,
    topped and tailed but not
    peeled
2 carrots, roughly chopped
4 celery stalks, roughly chopped
2 bay leaves
6 whole black peppercorns
handful of parsley stalks
scant 1 cup dry white wine
good splash of fino or manzanilla
    sherry, to serve

I have an obsession with consommés, those clear, glittering soups that pack a mighty flavour punch. They're what my wife would call "medicinal eating," the sort of food that leaves you glowing with health and feeling rather smug. It's becoming increasingly difficult to find a good canned consommé. Sainsbury's did a good version, but it seems it has moved on to the great recycling plant in the sky. Leaving me high and dry. Thank God, then, for Baxter's and Lusty's. Their beef consommés are crackers. But this recipe is very easy.

It also makes the base for a Bullshot. Heat the consommé and mix with Worcestershire sauce, Tabasco sauce, and the juice of half a lemon, then pour into glasses and mix with a measure of vodka. In summer, drink over ice.

Preheat the oven to 475°F. Put the oxtail and onions on a baking tray. Brown in the oven for 20 minutes.

Put the browned meat and onions into a big pot with the carrots, celery, bay leaves, peppercorns, and parsley stalks. Cover with about 2 quarts water (filtered if possible) and the wine. Bring to the boil, skim, then turn the heat down so there is the occasional blip rather than constant bubbling; do not let it boil.

Cook for about 4 hours, until the oxtail is very tender, topping up the water if need be. Strain into a bowl (reserving some shards of oxtail meat), cool, and put into the fridge overnight. It should set into a mass of gleaming brown jelly. Skim off the fat, then put the jelly into a pan and gently reheat. Taste and adjust the seasoning. Ladle into serving bowls with a few nuggets of meat and add a dash of sherry to taste.

Braised venison

Venison's a highly underrated meat and can range from the majestically rich (a well-hung red deer, say) to the subtle and sweet (muntjac, perhaps the finest of them all). Farmed deer are of a decent quality, and are probably the easiest to find in supermarkets. This recipe comes from my late stepmother, Rose.

To make the marinade, put all the ingredients into a pan, bring to a boil, then simmer for 3 minutes. Allow to cool.

Put the venison into a deep nonreactive bowl and cover with the marinade. Cover and marinate in the fridge for at least 24 hours (48 even better), turning occasionally.

Preheat the oven to 325°F. Remove the venison from the marinade and wipe dry with paper towels. Strain the marinade, reserving the bouquet garni, and set aside.

Heat the dripping in a large heavy-bottomed pan over a high heat and brown the meat all over. Remove and set aside. Reduce the heat slightly and in the same pan brown the onions, carrots, and celery. Put the venison back in the pan, along with the bouquet garni, strained marinade, and stock. Season, bring to a boil, then put into the oven for 2½–3 hours, until cooked and meltingly tender.

Transfer the venison to a carving board and slice. Strain the cooking liquid into a clean pan and skim, then add red currant jelly and whisk in the kneaded butter. Reduce by half, stir in the cream, then pour over the sliced venison. Serve with spiced red cabbage and mashed potatoes.

{ SERVES 4 }

3 pounds haunch of venison
1 tablespoon dripping, lard or
  goose fat
2 onions, finely chopped
2 carrots, finely chopped
2 celery stalks, finely chopped
1¼ cups chicken stock (cube OK)
1 teaspoon red currant jelly
kneaded butter (mix
  1 tablespoon plus 2 teaspoons
  unsalted butter with 2
  tablespoons all-purpose flour
  and knead until smooth)
2–3 tablespoons heavy cream

For the marinade
1 large onion, thinly sliced
1 large carrot, thinly sliced
1 celery stalk, thinly sliced
1 clove garlic
6 whole peppercorns
2 tablespoons olive oil
1 bouquet garni (2 bay leaves,
  1 sprig of celery leaves, 3 sprigs
  of thyme, 4 parsley leaves,
  stalks, and, if possible, roots,
  too; all tied together in a piece
  of cheesecloth)
1¼ cups red wine
2 tablespoons red wine vinegar
2 pieces of pared rind from an
  unwaxed lemon, as long as
  a little finger, chopped
pared rind of 1 orange
6 juniper berries, crushed

Proper ribs

{ SERVES 4–6 }
2⅛ cups cider vinegar

4⅜ pounds baby back
  pork ribs

For the dry rub

2 tablespoons hot paprika

2 tablespoons ground
  black pepper

2 tablespoons sea salt

1 teaspoon cayenne pepper

¼ cup muscovado sugar

2 tablespoons garlic powder

2 tablespoons onion powder

For the sauce

2 tablespoons unsalted butter

1 onion, finely chopped

4 garlic cloves, finely chopped

½ cup Bourbon

¾ cup tomato ketchup

⅓ cup plus 1 tablespoon dark
  brown sugar

¾ cup cider vinegar

1½ teaspoons English
  mustard powder

1 tablespoon soy sauce

2 teaspoons honey

1 tablespoon lemon juice

1 teaspoon chilli powder

½ teaspoon cayenne pepper

1 tablespoon Worcestershire
  sauce

½ teaspoon Tabasco sauce

I hadn't tasted proper ribs—the real, bone-sucking beauties, rather than those dried-up, mealy mouthed twigs that pass for ribs over here—until about seven years ago. I was a judge, one of many, at the Jack Daniel's Invitational Barbecue competition in Lynchburg, Tennessee. Two days were spent learning the ins and outs of professional pit judging—what garnishes were acceptable (green leaf lettuce, common curly parsley, and cilantro), how to tell if ribs were perfectly done ("When eating a properly cooked rib, the meat should come off the bone with very little effort and only where you bite into it should the meat be removed") and how to mark my meat (appearance, taste, and tenderness, one worst, nine impossibly brilliant). Before standing to take my oath to "truth, justice, excellence in barbecue, and the American way of life." With my right hand aloft, my eyes raised towards heaven.

Because in the south and southeast of America, barbecue does not mean abusing some perfectly innocent burger over a roaring flame. Real "que" is all about slow and low. Grilling is cooking over a direct heat. Barbecuing sees tough cuts of beef and pork smoked over an indirect heat for hours, until all those connective tissues are broken down into lusciously soft gelatin. As Lolis Eric Elie writes in *Smokestack Lightning* (Ten Speed Press, 2005) the "que" heads ". . . worship their own gods, they speak their own language, and they think that the ability to distinguish a brisket from a butt is no less basic to a civilized existence than are lounge chairs and chilled beer."

Once you're bitten by the bug, things get complicated pretty quickly. Oak or hickory, apple or cherry? Some pit masters like wet rubs, others dry. Texans love brisket, yet barbecue is predominantly pork—whole or hewn into various cuts. And as for the sauces . . . things get real fun here. In the west of North Carolina, pork shoulder is cooked over hickory or oak, then chopped or sliced and served with

{ CONTINUES OVERLEAF }

a tomato-based sauce. On the eastern side of the same state, barbecue means whole hog with a vinegar and pepper-spiked dressing. As Calvin Trillin wryly points out, "Americans argue not just about whose barbecue is second-best, but even what barbecue is about."

I use a Bradley Smoker for my ribs, a home smoker about the size of a mini bar. But the recipe below can be done in a classic kettle grill, too.

Mix 2 gallons plus 1½ quarts with the 2 cups vinegar, then soak the ribs in this mixture, covered and in the fridge, for 1 hour. Drain and dry with paper towels.

For the dry rub, mix all the ingredients together, then rub the mixture into the ribs (reserving the rest for later). Wrap in foil and leave in the fridge overnight.

To make the sauce, melt the butter in a saucepan over a medium heat and soften the onion and garlic. Add the Bourbon, then all the other ingredients, and cook at a gentle simmer for 30 minutes. Cover and set aside.

If using a Bradley Smoker, heat to 210°F, and use some hickory briquettes. Cook the ribs, wrapped in foil, on the top shelf for 1½ hours, then move to the bottom shelf for another 1½ hours. Take the ribs out and rub with the remaining dry rub, then cook on the top shelf for 1 hour and 45 minutes. Unwrap the foil, baste the ribs with sauce, rewrap, and cook on the bottom shelf for 45 minutes more.

If using a kettle barbecue, pile charcoal on one side of the base of the barbecue and put an old small roasting pan filled with water on a couple of bricks on the other side. Light the charcoal and heat until the coals are white-hot.

Sit the ribs, wrapped in the foil, on a rack over the water. Cover the barbecue with a lid, with the smoke holes half open. Use these holes to regulate the temperature, so when it begins to drop close the vents and open them when it gets very hot. Cook for 3 hours—you will need to top up the charcoal about every 40–60 minutes.

Rub the ribs with the remaining spice rub, rewrap in the foil, and return to the barbecue for another 2–3 hours until tender, topping up the charcoal from time to time. An hour before the end of the cooking time, open the foil and baste the ribs with the sauce.

When ready, the ribs should pull apart easily; the meat should not be falling off the bone but will come off cleanly when tugged by the teeth.

Pulled pork

A classic barbecue dish, taking a cheap shoulder of pork and cooking it at a low heat for hours until the meat can be cut with a spoon. In barbecue joints in the U.S., it's served with cheap white bread. The sauce is from east Carolina, spiked with vinegar and pepper, and cuts through the rich meat.

Mix all the ingredients for the dry rub and massage half the mixture into the pork. Wrap the pork in plastic wrap and leave in the fridge overnight.

The next day, remove the pork from the fridge, massage with the remaining dry rub, and let the pork come to room temperature.

If using a Bradley Smoker, heat to 200°F and cook the pork on one shelf from the bottom for 8 hours.

If using a kettle barbecue, soak one and one-half 1-pound packs of maple wood chips in a bucket of cold water as directed on the pack. Pile charcoal on one side of the base of the barbecue and put an old small roasting pan filled with cold water on a couple of bricks on the other side. Light the charcoal and leave until the coals are white. Sit the pork on foil with the edges folded up, then put it on the floating shelf (the shelf that is attached inside the lid) over the water, with a digital meat thermometer set to "pork" inserted into the meat (follow the manufacturer's instructions for using

{ CONTINUES OVERLEAF }

{ SERVES 6 }

1 (4–5-pound) rolled shoulder of
  pork

For the dry rub
1 ounce freshly ground black
  pepper
3 tablespoons hot paprika
1½ tablespoons demerara sugar
2 tablespoons sea salt
2 teaspoons English mustard
  powder
2 teaspoons cayenne pepper
2 teaspoons celery salt

**For the east Carolina
  vinegar sauce**
scant 2 cups cider vinegar
2 tablespoons brown sugar
2 teaspoons sea salt
1 teaspoon freshly ground black
  pepper
2 teaspoons hot chilli flakes or
  cayenne pepper

the thermometer). Scoop out a handful of soaked wood chips, add to the top of coals, and quickly shut the lid, with the smoke holes half open (see page 175). After 40 minutes, top up with more charcoal. After another 40–60 minutes, top up with more charcoal and a handful of drained wood chips. Keep the barbecue lid open for as short a time as possible so you don't lose heat or smoke. Cook for at least 6 hours (8 or 9 is better), checking every 40 minutes or so to ensure the heat is sufficient; top up with more charcoal when necessary.

Take out the pork and allow to cool slightly. Put all the ingredients for the sauce in a pan and heat gently, stirring, for long enough to dissolve the sugar. Serve with the meat.

Petit salé aux lentilles

A hale and hearty northern French dish, this is a recipe inspired by my friend Bill Knott, a fine cook and food writer. Sunday lunch at his house has been known to stretch well into Monday. Conversation may ebb and flow, but the stream of wine is continuous. This is also rather good cold.

Chop half the garlic into thick slivers and secrete them about the pork. Put the pork in a nonreactive container (or a strong plastic bag) and cover with sea salt. Add most of the thyme and scrunch it into the salt. Cover and leave in the fridge for 48–72 hours, turning when you remember.

Rinse the pork well in cold water. Put it in a pan, cover with cold water, and bring to a very gentle simmer. Add the bay and peppercorns and simmer, lid on, for 1½–2 hours over a low heat, until nearly tender, skimming occasionally. When the pork is cooked, remove it and strain and reserve the broth. When the meat is cool, remove the rib bones.

Heat the goose fat or olive oil in a big saucepan over a medium heat, then add the onions, carrots, and celery. Chop the rest of the garlic and chuck it in. Strip the leaves from the remaining thyme, chuck them in, then cook until the vegetables are soft but not browned.

Meanwhile, put the lentils in a saucepan, cover with cold water, bring to a boil, then drain them immediately and rinse them in hot water. Add them to the vegetables, then add the pork and enough of the reserved broth to cover the meat. Cover the pan and simmer very gently for 30–40 minutes, or until the lentils and pork are tender.

Cut the pork into thick slices. Reduce the lentils a little over a high heat, if needed, then stir in the mustard and parsley, check the seasoning, and spoon into a serving dish. Arrange the pork on top, and eat with crusty bread and more mustard.

{ SERVES 6 }

6 garlic cloves

3–4-pound slab of pork belly, fairly lean, bones in

copious coarse sea salt (¾–1 pound)

bunch of thyme

3 whole bay leaves

12 whole black peppercorns

3 tablespoons goose fat or olive oil

3 onions, roughly chopped

3 carrots, peeled and roughly chopped

2 celery stalks, roughly chopped

2¼ cups Puy lentils

3 tablespoons smooth Dijon mustard, plus extra to serve

big bunch of flat-leaf parsley, finely chopped

crusty bread, to serve

Penne all'amatriciana

3 tablespoons olive oil

1⅓ pounds smoked pancetta,
   cut into strips, about
   ¼ inch thick and 1½ inches
   long

4 red onions, finely chopped

big pinch of dried peperoncino
   or dried chilli flakes or
   2–5 dried bird's-eye chillies,
   finely chopped

3 large sprigs of rosemary,
   stripped and finely chopped

1 cup red wine

2 (28-ounce) cans chopped
   tomatoes

sea salt and freshly ground
   black pepper

4½ ounces Parmesan, grated,
   plus extra to serve

1 pound dried penne

This is one of the first dishes I cooked regularly after leaving university, and was a stalwart when having girls over for dinner. It took a couple of hours, smelt wondrous, and tasted divine. It also gave time for a few glasses of wine. This was all about seduction via the stomach.

Heat the oil in a large heavy-bottomed saucepan over a medium–high heat and fry the pancetta until crisp. Reduce the heat to medium, add the onions, and cook for about 10 minutes, until soft. Add the chilli and rosemary and cook for 2 minutes.

Chuck in the wine and increase the heat to burn off the alcohol; stir to deglaze the pan. Add the tomatoes and check the seasoning.

Turn down the heat to very low and cook, lid off, at a very slow blip for 2½–3 hours, until the sauce is thick and dry. Stir more frequently towards the end of cooking as the sauce thickens. Add grated Parmesan.

Cook the penne according to the package instructions. Drain and mix with the sauce (don't overwhelm with sauce; the pasta should have equal billing) and serve immediately. Grate over some more Parmesan if you like.

Greek-style roast lamb with macaroni

{ SERVES 4 }

1 (2¼-pound) lamb shoulder, cut into 4, with the bone left in (ask your butcher to chop the lamb)

1 small lemon, halved

sea salt and freshly ground black pepper

1 tablespoon all-purpose flour, seasoned

2 tablespoons olive oil

2¼ pounds fresh or canned tomatoes, roughly chopped

1 cup dry white wine

2 tablespoons tomato purée

3 whole cloves

1 cinnamon stick, broken

For the macaroni

3¾ cups full-fat milk

11 tablespoons (1 stick plus 3 tablespoons) unsalted butter, plus extra for greasing

½ cup plus 1 tablespoon all-purpose flour

1 egg yolk

1 pound long Greek macaroni

3 egg whites

4½ ounces *kefalotyri* or Pecorino cheese, grated

½ cup breadcrumbs, toasted

The Greeks are masters of lamb. And one of my favourite lunches of the year is at Greek Easter. I go to my friend Noli's house (well, his parents', anyway), and they roast a whole lamb on the spit as well as making an epic tripe soup. This recipe is more practical than the first, and less polarizing than the second. It has a subtle spicing and real depth. If you can't find long Greek macaroni, look for the Italian equivalent. Or even normal macaroni if desperate, although the aesthetic effect is somewhat lost.

Preheat the oven to 300°F. Rub the lamb with the lemon, squeezing over the juice and reserving the rinds, and season. Cover and put in the fridge to marinate for 15–20 minutes. Dice the lemon rinds and set aside. Dust the lamb with seasoned flour. Heat the olive oil in a heavy roasting pan over a medium–high heat, add the lamb and brown it all over. Add the tomatoes and cook until bubbling.

Mix the wine with the tomato purée and add to the lamb, followed by the cloves, cinnamon, and diced lemon rind. Pour in enough water (about ⅔ cup) to cover the meat. Loosely cover the pan with foil and bake in the oven for 2½–3 hours, until the meat is falling off the bone.

After 1½–2 hours cooking, make the sauce for the macaroni. Warm the milk in a saucepan. In a separate saucepan, melt 5 tablespoons of the butter over a low heat until foaming.

{ CONTINUES OVERLEAF }

Add the flour a little at a time, whisking, until smooth. Remove from the heat.

Slowly add the warm milk, whisking continuously to prevent lumps forming. Place the sauce back over a low heat and cook for 3–4 minutes, stirring often, until it has thickened to the consistency of cream.

Remove the sauce from the heat and season. Lightly whisk the egg yolk and beat it into the sauce. Set aside.

Lightly butter a large, shallow baking dish. Bring a large pot of salted water to a boil and cook the macaroni for half the time recommended on the package. Drain and lay it out on a baking sheet.

Melt the remaining butter in a small saucepan. In a bowl, whisk the egg whites until fluffy. Stir in half the melted butter, then pour this mixture over the macaroni, turning to coat evenly.

Put a thin layer of sauce in the bottom of the prepared baking dish. Sprinkle with a little cheese, then add a layer of macaroni. Sprinkle with more cheese, and a little more sauce and another layer of macaroni. Repeat until all the macaroni and sauce have been used. Sprinkle over the remaining cheese, then sprinkle over the breadcrumbs and top with the rest of the melted butter.

Thirty minutes before the lamb is ready, turn up the oven to 400°F. Remove the foil from the lamb to brown the meat and reduce the juices in the pan to a rich, sticky sauce. Bake the macaroni on the top shelf of the oven for 30 minutes, or until golden brown and crisp on top. Serve alongside the lamb.

Shoulder of lamb with pommes boulangère

{ SERVES 4 }

4 large onions, about
   1⅓ pounds, thinly sliced
big bunch of thyme
sea salt and freshly ground
   black pepper
2¾ pounds Idaho potatoes,
   sliced into ½-inch-thick rounds
1 whole shoulder of lamb,
   3½–4½ pounds, excess fat
   removed
1 tablespoon Gentleman's Relish
1 head garlic, separated into
   cloves, peeled
10–12 small sprigs of rosemary
5 cups hot chicken stock (cubes
   OK, but home-made better)

This really does require the minimum of preparation, but dear God, it's good. The lamb sits atop a tray of potatoes wallowing in stock, mixed with onion and a little thyme. As the meat cooks, slow and low, the juices infuse into the broth. You'll end up with lamb that disintegrates very pleasingly, and some of the most seductive potatoes you'll ever meet. You want to slice the potatoes about ½ inch thick, so they keep some shape at the end. A mandoline does make things a lot easier, but a knife will do.

As for the Gentleman's Relish, don't panic. Some people hate the stuff, others worship it. The Victorians and Edwardians couldn't get enough anchovy butter and essence. Anchovies and lamb are natural bedfellows and, once the heat hits the relish, it loses any fishy aggression (like Southeast Asian fish sauce) and adds a wonderful umami-infused extra level of flavour.

⎯⎯⎯⎯

Preheat the oven to 300°F.

Take a large Le Creuset-type rectangular dish (Pyrex is fine, too) and fill with a layer of onions, then sprinkle with thyme, salt, and pepper. Then add a layer of potatoes, making sure they cover the onions. Repeat the layers of onions, thyme, seasoning, and potatoes until everything is used up, ending up with a layer of potatoes.

Make 10–12 slits in the lamb. Shove a smear of Gentleman's Relish, a clove of garlic, and a small sprig of rosemary into each slit, until all the holes are filled and the shoulder resembles a Tim Burton hedgehog. Season.

Pour the stock over the potatoes and onions, until just covered. Put the shoulder of lamb on top and bake, uncovered, in the oven for 4 hours, or until cooked.

Rabbit & cider casserole

Wild rabbits. Millions of the buggers, infesting the countryside, yet the vast majority of us shy away, seeing them as a "difficult" meat alongside other game. But they have a mild flavour and excellent texture, though they do tend towards dryness. Wild are the best and any decent butcher should be able to get hold of them. He'll also joint them for you. They're cheap, too. Farmed rabbits are available but have all the depth of a baking sheet. This is a dish with a proper West Country burr, to be accompanied by a dry cider, preferably from Burrow Hill in Somerset.

{ SERVES 4 }

7 tablespoons all-purpose flour
sea salt and freshly ground
    black pepper
2 rabbits (wild, if possible),
    jointed
2 tablespoons olive oil
2 tablespoons unsalted butter
1 onion, roughly chopped
1 bay leaf
2 sprigs thyme
1²⁄₃ cups good dry cider
2⅛ cups chicken stock
3 tablespoons heavy cream
small handful curly parsley,
    roughly chopped
steamed cabbage with crisp
    cooked bacon and mashed
    potatoes, to serve

Season 4 tablespoons of the flour generously, then roll the rabbit pieces in it, shaking off any excess. Heat the oil in a heavy-bottomed enamelled casserole over a medium–high heat and fry the rabbit for 5 minutes, turning once or twice, until golden brown. Remove from the pan and drain on paper towels.

Add the butter to the pan, then tip in the onion. Reduce the heat to medium and fry the onion for 10 minutes until softened and golden. Stir in the remaining 3 tablespoons flour, then add the bay leaf and thyme. Gradually pour in the cider and chicken stock, stirring continuously. Increase the heat to high and bring to a boil, stirring.

Return the rabbit to the casserole, taste, and season. Cover, then reduce the heat to low, and simmer for about 2 hours, or until the meat is tender and almost falling off the bone. (Alternatively, transfer the casserole to an oven preheated to 300°F for 2 hours.)

Using a slotted spoon, remove the rabbit from the casserole and set aside on a warm plate. Pour the cream into the casserole and simmer gently for a few minutes until slightly thicker. Return the rabbit to the casserole, along with any juices, then adjust the seasoning and sprinkle over the parsley. Serve with the cabbage and mashed potatoes.

{ From far-flung shores }

These are recipes gleaned from ten years of travelling in total thrall to my gut. My tastes are resolutely low. Give me decent street food over the most elaborate of Michelin-starred confections. It's no coincidence that two of my favourite cuisines in the world, Mexican and Thai, have the most thriving pavement tucker you'll find anywhere. Many of the recipes in this chapter are adapted street-food dishes, and while you'll never be able to replicate sitting outside a Mexico City *taquería* munching on *tacos al pastor*, or perching on a wobbly plastic stool in Bangkok while wolfing down green papaya salad, I hope they give a decent approximation.

Don't be put off by the long lists of strange ingredients, or the sometimes seemingly endless preparation needed. Nothing is overly difficult or elaborate, and nothing requires any specific skill beyond handling a knife or pounding with a pestle and mortar. The cooking is the easiest bit of all. Once the prep is in place, the rest is a cinch. And in our bold new digital age, even the most obscure of shrimp pastes and Central American herbs are but a click away.

{ Chillies }

You may have noticed that chillies play a starring role in many of my recipes. I love these pungent pods in their every form, bow down to their versatile brilliance, worship at the altar of capsaicin, the irritant that gives chillies their heat.

It all started with my first taste of a Madras curry. Before long, I was after bigger kicks, getting mired deeper and deeper into a dangerous and pulse-quickening world. Vindaloo came next, and I rarely travelled without a bottle of Tabasco close to hand. Thai soups and salads followed, the sort that bead the forehead in sweat and render any conversation impossible. From there, it was a slippery slope to sinister-sounding hot sauces—Blair's Ultra Death, Da' Bomb, Dave's Insanity. And before I knew it, I was subscribing to *Chile Pepper Magazine*, growing my own Scotch bonnets, and scouring the streets late at night, desperate for a hit of something fierce and red.

There's no doubt that chillies are addictive. Sure, there's pain, often wave after wave of it, enough to bring you to your knees. Once, a few years back, I went to the National Fiery Foods Show in Albuquerque, New Mexico. Emboldened by a few beers, I decided to try one particular sauce that came in at two million on the Scoville scale (this measures chilli heat—Tabasco sits around 5,000). So this extract sauce (meaning it uses chemically extracted capsaicin, the same thing you'd find in pepper spray), called something like Exquisite Agony, was fierce. I tasted only the tiniest amount, enough to cover the head of a pin. But dear God, did it hurt. So much so that I hit the ground, bent double, my tongue a useless, throbbing mass of dead flesh, my throat aflame, my whole nervous system in revolt. Even thinking pained me. Then came the endorphins, released to fight the pain, charging in like valiant troopers to quash the infidel horde. And slowly, very slowly, I came back to life. What followed was that soft, toasty afterburn, where colours seemed sharper, sounds amplified, and smells became that much more vivid. This experience, to a greater or lesser extent, has been repeated all over the world, from Thai markets to Mexican cantinas. My wife just shakes her head, while friends are so used to my grunting and sweating that they just carry on eating, regardless.

But chillies are not all about heat. They're about flavour, too. That's why I love the food of Mexico, India, and Thailand. The fresh habaneros and bird's-eye chillies are fiercely hot, but they have their own character, too. And there's a world of difference between the green kick of a jalapeño and the mild appeal of a banana chilli. When dried, many chillies become more complex and rich—the serious, smoky heft of the chipotle (a smoked dried

'Before I knew it, I was subscribing to Chile Pepper Magazine, growing my own Scotch Bonnets and scouring the streets late at night, desperate for a hit of something fierce and red.'

jalapeño), the sharp charm of the ancho, the chocolate warmth of the mulato. Depending on your tastes, you can adjust the level of heat in the recipes to your liking.

And despite my love for the chilli, I'm not so obsessed that I would use it out of context. I don't douse Yorkshire puddings with Caribbean hot sauce, nor do I spike my ragù alla Bolognese with Hungarian hot wax. That said, a week without heat and my body starts craving. The chilli is unquestionably the greatest of all fruits, the ingredient I love above all other. A life spent without it would be very dull indeed.

Top row from left: jalapeño and Thai bird's-eye chillies
Second row from left: cayenne, habaneros, chipotle meco, chipotle morita
Bottom row from left: ancho, Thai dried red chillies, and chipotle morita

{ Thai food }

The best lunches often occur in the most incongruous of places. It was just after noon, deep in the *khlongs* (canals) of Bangkok. The sun beat down and all was languid, save the occasional put-put of river-boats selling noodles, chillies, and herbs in every hue of green.

We were with David Thompson, one of the world's great Thai chefs and the author of *Thai Food* (Pavilion, 2002), the finest work on this cuisine in the English language. And we were hungry. Suddenly, without warning, he tells the boat driver to stop. We pull up at a makeshift pontoon, where a noodle seller is bent over bubbling pots. You choose your noodles and whatever you want on top—fish balls, chicken, or prawns—then everything is covered with a rich pork broth. You add fish sauce, or fresh chilli, or dried chilli powder to taste ("Every dish in Thailand is personalized at the table," says David, "a touch of sugar, a handful of chillies, whatever.") and dig in.

The lunch was simplicity itself, but every element was divine—the broth clean, fresh, and fragrant, and the noodles made that morning, still slightly chewy. A squeeze of lime for a citrus kick, the chillies' fierce, floral heat. I just kept eating, bowl after bowl. This was food as it should be, glorious, cheap, and unpretentious. Sweating with joy and chilli heat, I ask David how many times he'd

famous? He shook his head. "Never been here before. But this is Thailand. They're obsessed with food. If it wasn't any good, it would be gone in days."

The next few days were spent in a wanton orgy of eating. Oyster omelettes, frazzled at the bottom, gooey on top. Fish-gut curries fierce and sinister; slightly fermented pork sausages, plump and tart, green papaya salads so hot that time seemed to slow down and you entered a capsaicin-fuelled nether world of pain and pleasure.

"Food is the only democratic institution in Thailand," David told us en route to yet another feast. "It's a unifying force. Thai food from region to region is as distinct as that of Italy or France. They don't much care about politics. The only time there are real riots is when the rice is too expensive. When they're not eating, they're thinking about what they're going to eat, or working out where they'll eat. When in bed, they'll dream about it. Good food is not just a luxury for the rich. Thai people really do eat to live and live to eat."

Balance is everything: of the hot, sweet, salty, and sour. Some dishes will just use two of these elements, while others will use three or four. But Thai cooking is all about the juggling of ingredients and disparate, often potent, flavours to create one harmo

In Bangkok and the central plains region, with its historic wealth and countless outside influences, dishes can be complex. The many rivers provide abundant prawns, catfish, and crabs, and hot and salty is probably the dominant taste. This is the home of sour orange curries and fiery *tom yam gung* (hot-and-sour prawn soup). The street food has a strong Chinese influence.

In the north, plain rice becomes sticky, coconuts are rare, and shrimp paste nowhere near as important to cooking as it is in the central plains—although hot and salty rules here, too. Pork is king; game and various reptiles are eaten. *Kao soi*, a curried noodle dish with roots in China, is a speciality of Chiang Mai. And the Chiang Mai sausage, slightly sour, is another favourite.

The northeast, or Isarn region, was traditionally isolated, with many different ethnic groups. The region is poor and predominantly rural, the food very hot. Less food to dress the rice means more intensity of flavour, heat, and pungency is needed. Various versions of *larp*, a salad of minced meat or fish, are popular, as they are in neighbouring Laos. There's also all manner of insects (ant-egg soup is pretty good), snakes, and jungle cats. People here have little time for Western squeamishness, rather eating whatever they can to survive. Thailand's south has vivid, almost gaudy, food, and dried bird's-eye chillies reign supreme. There's lots of coconut, fruit in the curries, and, of course, seafood.

In Britain, Thai food is pretty dire. Everything seems overly sweet, deep-fried, and emasculated, as if all the interesting parts—the shrimp paste with its tang of the sewer, the chilli heat, the elegance and balance of flavours—are too much for our tender palates. Thompson's view is that the Thai people are so hospitable that they give us what they think we want, rather than cooking as they do at home. And he's right. Armed with this knowledge, I marched into my local Thai and demanded, politely, the food they were eating. At first, they ignored the *farang* (foreigner) and smiled sweetly. But I persisted. And suddenly they relented, and the food came alive. I was eating proper Thai food, minutes away from Bayswater tube.

The recipes here are all classics, some of it street food (which is mainly Chinese in origin), some home cooking. All, though, make the senses sing. If you don't like the chillies, cut the quantity down. The dried ones have a slow-burning heat, while the fresh scuds are lethal but utterly addictive. As ever, fiddle until you find what you like. They may not all be entirely authentic. But compared to the usual lifeless pap served up in the name of Thai food, they're a whole new world of edible delight.

Thai beef salad

This is a classic of Thai cookery; incredibly simple to make but it does take a little preparation for the chilli and rice powders. I tend to make them both in big batches and store them in an airtight box or bottle. With these at hand, the dish can be made in moments. It mixes the sour with the hot, and the rice powder gives a wonderful golden crunch.

Mix the shallots with the herbs and divide between 2 plates.

Rub the steak with a little oil and season. Preheat a griddle pan to hot and cook the steak for 2 minutes on each side, then leave to rest for 2 minutes. Slice it thinly and lay the slices on top of the herbs and shallots.

To make the dressing, mix together the fish sauce, lime juice, and roasted chilli powder. Pour over the salad, then sprinkle with the roasted rice powder.

{ **Roasted chilli powder** } Heat a small heavy-based pan to smoking hot and dry-fry 6 dried, long Thai chillies for about 1 minute—open the windows as the fumes could bring down an elephant. Remove from the heat, leave to cool, and grind the chillies to a powder using a pestle and mortar.

{ **Roasted rice powder** } Heat a small heavy-based pan over a medium–low heat and dry-fry uncooked white sticky rice for 2–3 minutes, until the rice starts to toast and give off a wonderful burnished biscuity smell. Crush using a pestle and mortar.

{ SERVES 2 }

6 Thai shallots, thinly sliced
good handful each of mint, cilantro, and holy basil leaves
1 pound thick-cut sirloin steak
vegetable oil
sea salt and freshly ground black pepper

For the dressing
3 tablespoons fish sauce
⅓ cup lime juice
2 big pinches of roasted chilli powder (*see* method)
1 tablespoon roasted rice powder (*see* method)

Stir-fried beef with cumin

{ SERVES 2 }

⅔ pound trimmed beef rump
2 tablespoons fish sauce
big pinch of roasted chilli
  powder (*see* page 199)
8 dried red chillies, toasted
3 tablespoons peanut oil
1½ heaped tablespoons cumin
  and chilli paste (see below)
1 teaspoon palm or superfine
  sugar
2 teaspoons rice wine vinegar
4 teaspoons tamarind water
  (*see* page 206)
1 red onion, cut into wedges
bunch of cilantro,
  roughly chopped
steamed rice, to serve

For the cumin and chilli paste
2 teaspoons cumin seeds
6 dried red Thai chillies,
  seeded and soaked in
  warm water for 30 minutes,
  then drained
½ teaspoon sea salt
5 Thai shallots, finely chopped
6 garlic cloves, finely chopped

I've hugely adapted this recipe from David Thompson and I'm sure he—and Matthew Albert, his equally talented head chef at Nahm in London—would be appalled. Like all Thai food, there's a bit of preparation involved. But the end result is quick to cook and well worth the effort.

First, make the cumin and chilli paste. Heat a small pan over low to medium heat, add the cumin seeds, and dry-fry until fragrant. Leave to cool, then grind using a pestle and mortar or electric spice grinder. Pound the chillies and salt together using a pestle and mortar, then add the shallots, garlic, and 1 teaspoon of the freshly ground cumin (reserve the rest for the beef); grind to a paste. This will make about 4 tablespoons; keep whatever you don't use in the fridge for up to 3 days.

Cut the beef into thin slices across the grain. Mix the fish sauce, roasted chilli powder, and remaining ground cumin in a bowl, add the whole dried toasted chillies and the beef. Coat the beef in the marinade, cover, and leave to marinate in the fridge for 30 minutes.

Heat the oil in a wok until smoking, then take the beef and whole chillies out of the marinade and fry until the beef colours, 1–2 minutes. Add 1½ heaped tablespoons of the cumin and chilli paste, breaking it up and stirring until it becomes fragrant. Then add the sugar, vinegar, and tamarind water and simmer for 1 minute. Taste. It should be hot, salty, and rich with cumin—a little sticky, too.

Remove from the heat and stir through the red onion quarters and cilantro. Serve with steamed rice.

Minced beef with chillies & basil

A Thai street-food staple, although a relatively recent one. Of course, you'll never be able to replicate the smoky tinge that comes from a veteran, battle-scarred street wok. But this has it all—slightly frazzled beef, oozing fried egg, the ubiquitous chilli, and the clovey, slightly tongue-numbing holy basil. Get the best beef you can afford, preferably coarsely minced sirloin.

Finely chop the garlic with a pinch of salt and the chillies.

Add half the oil to a wok or frying pan and heat until smoking. Fry the eggs, then set aside and keep warm.

To make the dipping sauce, mix the fish sauce, garlic, and chillies. Set aside. Just before serving, add the lime juice and cilantro.

Add the remaining oil to the wok or pan, heat until smoking, then fry the garlic and chilli mixture for a few moments. Add the beef and cook for 1 minute, then add the fish sauce and sugar.

Add the stock and simmer for a few seconds, then stir in the basil. Divide between 2 bowls and top with a fried egg. Serve with steamed white rice and the dipping sauce.

{ SERVES 2 }

3 garlic cloves, peeled

salt

3–10 bird's-eye chillies

3 tablespoons peanut oil

2 eggs

⅔ pound ground beef

1 tablespoon fish sauce

large pinch of granulated sugar

1 tablespoon chicken stock

2 large handfuls holy basil leaves

steamed Thai fragrant rice,
  to serve

For the dipping sauce

¼ cup fish sauce

1 garlic clove, finely sliced

3–10 bird's-eye chillies,
  finely chopped

2 tablespoons lime juice

pinch of fresh cilantro, finely
  chopped

Spicy pork balls

{ SERVES 4 }

2 chillies, preferably Thai
  bird's-eye, finely sliced
½ lemongrass stalk
small handful of cilantro,
  ideally with roots, finely
  chopped
handful of mint, finely chopped
handful of Thai basil, finely
  chopped
good pinch of freshly ground
  black pepper
generous ¾ pound free-range
  ground pork
2 tablespoons peanut oil
2 iceberg lettuces, leaves
  separated, to serve

For the dipping sauce
4 bird's-eye chillies, finely
  chopped
1 garlic clove, thinly sliced
pinch of superfine sugar
2 tablespoons lime juice
1 tablespoon fish sauce

This Thai dish is good for a snack or starter. It's hard to find minced free-range pork from the butcher, but do search it out. It's far preferable to the insipid supermarket stuff. The herbs, as ever, lift the dish from the everyday to the exquisite, while the iceberg lettuce, much maligned, adds cool crunch.

Crush the chillies, lemongrass, herbs, and black pepper with a pestle and mortar or a blender. Mix well with the minced pork.

Shape the mixture into about 20 small balls (wet your hands so the mixture doesn't stick).

Heat the oil in a frying pan over a medium heat and fry the balls all over for 8–10 minutes, until cooked inside. Cut one in half; it should be evenly coloured with no traces of pink— if not, cook for a little longer. Drain on paper towels.

To make the dipping sauce, combine the chillies, garlic, sugar, lime juice, and fish sauce in a small bowl.

Pile the pork balls on a plate and serve with the lettuce leaves and dipping sauce.

Larp gai (Laotian chicken salad)

It took mere minutes to fall in love with Laos, that landlocked Southeast Asian country still scarred by the Vietnam War. Overshadowed by its immediate neighbours, China and Burma to the north, Vietnam to the east, Cambodia to the south, and Thailand to the west, it's one of the world's few remaining Communist states. Not that this bothers the residents, who are some of the most open and hospitable people I've ever met. Vientiane has to be the most laid-back capital in the world. Even the traffic lights change at languorous pace. And Luang Phrabang, the ancient royal capital, is better still, dreamily tranquil and endlessly beautiful, studded with temples and cut through by the mighty Mekong River.

It's a poor country, with many living way below the poverty line. In rural areas you'll find markets selling jungle cats and frogs, snakes, insects, even dried rats. The water beetles, great fat beasts, were rather good, with a taste of pear drops. And the deep-fried bee pupae were far superior to the dullard peanut as a bar snack. But it's *larp* (or *larb*) I ate the most: pretty much the national dish, it's a riot of tastes and textures. Traditionally made with minced water buffalo meat; rather hard to come by in the local supermarket—you can use minced pork, or, as in this recipe, chicken instead.

{ SERVES 2 }

⅔ cup chicken stock

big pinch of sugar (palm if possible but superfine is fine)

¾ pound chicken breast, minced by hand

⅓ cup lime juice

2 tablespoons fish sauce

4–5 bird's-eye chillies, chopped

2 large pinches of roasted chilli powder (*see* page 199)

5 Thai shallots, thinly sliced

handful of mint, coarsely chopped

handful of cilantro, finely chopped

2 large pinches of roasted fine rice powder (*see* page 199)

Combine the stock and sugar in a saucepan and bring to a simmer. Add the chicken and simmer gently for 5–10 minutes, or until cooked through.

Remove from the heat and add the lime juice, fish sauce, chillies, chilli powder, shallots, and herbs.

Sprinkle with the roasted rice powder and serve.

Chicken, lime, & lemongrass soup

{ SERVES 2 }

2 quarts fresh chicken stock (*see* page 38), boiled to reduce to 4 cups

2 lemongrass stalks, bruised

4 slices of galangal, each about the size of a quarter

9 Thai shallots, peeled

2 chicken breasts (the best you can afford)

6 tablespoons lime juice

3–4 tablespoons fish sauce

big pinch of bird's-eye chillies, finely chopped

1 tablespoon lemongrass, finely chopped

handful of cilantro, roughly chopped, to garnish

A deeply soothing, medicinal broth. It's incredibly easy to make, although you do need good stock. You get waves of lime, lemongrass, and galangal that all work in heavenly harmony. A dish we eat pretty much every week. It builds layer upon layer of flavour. Marinating the cooked chicken in the fish sauce and lime base gives an extra level of zing.

Put the stock in a large pan, bring to a simmer, and add the lemongrass stalks, galangal, and 3 whole shallots. Simmer for 10 minutes.

Add the chicken breasts, cover, and simmer for 10–12 minutes more, or until they are cooked through. Turn off the heat, remove the chicken, leave to cool, and then shred. Strain the stock, discarding the aromatics.

Slice the remaining 6 shallots. Divide the shredded chicken between 2 bowls and add 3 tablespoons of lime juice and 1½–2 tablespoons of the fish sauce to each. Add the shallots, chillies, and lemongrass and set aside for 20 minutes.

Reheat the stock until boiling, pour over the chicken, and mix. Finish with a handful of chopped cilantro.

Green papaya salad

{ SERVES 2 OR 4
AS A SIDE DISH }

3 garlic cloves, peeled

sea salt

1 heaped teaspoon roasted
  peanuts, crushed

2 tablespoons dried
  prawns (optional)

4 cherry tomatoes, quartered

5 green beans, sliced into
  ½-inch lengths

5 bird's-eye chillies

½ pound green papaya,
  shredded

2 tablespoons palm or
  superfine sugar

1 tablespoon lime juice

1 tablespoon tamarind water
  (see below)

2 tablespoons fish sauce

steamed Thai rice, to serve

Chinese cabbage, quartered,
  to serve

I'll never forget my first bite. I was eighteen, greener than a young papaya, and in Bangkok for the first time. Having just spent six months in the Indian wilderness, arriving in the garish, neon-soaked Thai capital was like that moment where Dorothy arrives in Oz, and the screen changes from monochrome to glorious Technicolor. Anyway, the first street-food vendor I found (or plucked up the courage to approach) was selling a sort of greeny-white salad in a bag. I did a lot of pointing and nodding and was asked, "How hot?" Chest puffed up, I answered, "Thai hot. Like you." He smiled, but did as I asked. The first bite was astonishing. The crunch of green papaya, the saline chew of dried shrimps, a tang of lime, and a mouth-puckering hit of tamarind. Then the chillies took hold, coming in wave after wave, increasing in ferocity until even my brain throbbed in pain. I had to sit down, head in hand, hyperventilating. The vendors howled with laughter. Once the pain had subsided, though, I wanted more.

Pound the garlic with a pinch of salt using a pestle and mortar. Add the peanuts and dried prawns and continue pounding to a coarse paste. Add the tomatoes and beans, pounding lightly. Add the chillies. The more you pound them, the more oils disperse and the hotter it gets. So beware.

Put the shredded papaya in a large bowl, add the chilli mixture, and continue to bruise and mix with the pestle. Season with the sugar, lime, tamarind water, and fish sauce. Serve with rice and Chinese cabbage.

{ **Tamarind water** } If you can get fresh tamarind, pull off a few sticky buds and put them in warm water for 5 minutes. Mulch between your fingertips, then push through a sieve. Alternatively, soak 1 teaspoon dried tamarind in 2 tablespoons boiling water for 5 minutes, then strain through a fine sieve.

Shrimp broth

When I first tried this, deep in Soho on a dull Sunday afternoon, I was rendered speechless. It had such intensity, and depth, from relatively few basic ingredients. To re-create it, I used dried shrimps from a Chinese supermarket and they worked just fine. Guajillo chillies are dried chillies with a mild flavour, or try using about 4–6 dried bird's-eye chillies. Totally different flavour, but works well.

Put the shrimps in a saucepan, add 2 quarts water, bring to a boil, then simmer for 15 minutes.

Meanwhile, toast the chillies in a dry frying pan until fragrant, then soak them in boiling water for 20 minutes, until soft.

Heat the vegetable oil in a saucepan. Add the onions and soften over a medium heat for 5 minutes. Add the celery, carrots, parsley sprigs, and avocado leaves, if using. Cook for 15 minutes. Add the potatoes for the last 4 minutes.

When the shrimp cooking time is up, remove them from the broth with a slotted spoon and set aside. Strain the broth into a container. In a blender, purée the soaked chillies with a tablespoon of the shrimps.

Return the broth to the pan, add the softened vegetables, stir in the shrimps and shrimp-chilli paste, and simmer for 10 minutes more. Serve with quartered limes.

{ SERVES 8 }

⅔ pound dried shrimps
3 guajillo chillies, seeded and opened out
1 tablespoon vegetable oil
2 white onions, finely chopped
1 small celery stalk, finely chopped
5 carrots, cut into cubes
3 sprigs flat-leaf parsley
3 avocado leaves (optional)
4 waxy potatoes, peeled and cut into cubes
6 limes, quartered

{ Mexican food }

Why is it that Mexican food has such a wretched reputation in the UK? After all, this is a Titan among cuisines, astonishingly varied and endlessly exciting. From the lip-tingling ceviches of Baja California to *mole negro* in Oaxaca, Jaliscan whole grilled fish, naked save a squeeze of lime, to pig heaven with Yucatán *cochinita pibil*—not forgetting *tacos al pastor* in Mexico City, among a thousand other culinary delights—this vast country has it all.

The Mexicans are masters of the chilli, using it fresh and dried for heat and flavour. Some, such as the fresh *poblano* and dried *pasilla*, are mild and rich. Others, like the fruit-scented habanero, can take off the top of your head.

At the heart of everything is corn, which we know as maize. The smell of cooking *masa* dough (maize slaked with calcium hydroxide or lime) is the scent of Mexico. Tacos, the soft corn tortillas, are ubiquitous, but there are myriad ways with this most essential of ingredients: *gordas* (griddled pockets), *sopes* (small fried disks), *chalupas*, *memelas*, *picadas*, *quesadillas*, *panuchos*. The Mexicans are food fanatics, stopping at any opportunity for a crisp *flauta*, stuffed with pork, or a shrimp taco, or *quesadilla*. This is a culture built around eating.

So how come the British see Mexican food as greasy, tasteless, and turgid, with a tendency to squat in the belly like a cheese-coated shot put? "Tex-Mex," that's why, a nauseating blend of bad mariachi music, second-rate Tequila, and sizzling platters of, well, I'm not sure what.

Anyone brave enough to venture into their local "Break For the Border," "Sombreros and Slammers," or "Greedy Gonzales" takes their digestive well-being into very dangerous territory. The guacamole is slopped from a vast catering pack, made months before and kept alive with a noxious cocktail of preservatives and colourings. The salsa comes straight from a jar, purse-lipped and mean, while the tortilla chips are little more than Doritos from the wrong side of the tracks. There are comedy cocktails in comedy glasses that stain the tongue in comedy colours and frozen margaritas sold by the foot. Along with bargain-basement chilli con carnes (not a Mexican dish, despite what these places might claim) with humorous names ("Ring of Fire," etc), overrun with beans and cheap mince. Everything comes buried in a slick of greasy, microwave-nuked cheese, even the puddings.

As you stagger out of the door, senses numbed and sweating despair, you vow never, ever, to eat "Mexican" again. Of course, this is no more Mexican than Pizza Hut is Italian. But it matters not. The damage has been done. And this fine and mighty cuisine suffers another unwarranted blow, sullied and horribly debased.

It's not just the food that suffers from bad PR, but the whole country. Most people believe that Mexico is a war zone, with bullets sprayed willy-nilly and bodies piled waist high. There *is* a catastrophic narco war going on in the north, by the U.S. border, and occasionally the violence spills out to Acapulco, or Mexico City. But Mexico is far more sinned against than sinning. And it's one of my favourite countries in the world.

I've been a dozen times, and always want to return. The smell of cooking corn, petrol fumes, grilling beef, and roasting chillies. Bliss.

Some of these recipes come from my friend Alberto, a fantastic chef and native of Mexico City, with whom I've cooked on a couple of occasions. He is a master, I'm a mere apprentice. This is just a taste, but enough, I hope, to prove that Mexican food is many miles removed from that filth the British call "Tex-Mex."

'The smell of cooking corn, Petrol fumes, grilling beef and roasting Chillies. Bliss.'

Mexican beef stew

{ SERVES 4 }

2 tablespoons olive oil

2 pounds braising steak or shin,
  cut into 1-inch cubes

2 onions, roughly chopped

2 garlic cloves, finely chopped

1-pound 9-ounce jar of passata

2 tablespoons red wine vinegar

3–8 chipotles (soaked in warm
  water for 15 minutes,
  stemmed and finely chopped)

2 bay leaves

1 teaspoon dried Mexican
  oregano (European oregano
  would work, too)

sea salt

To serve

fresh corn tortillas

big bunch of cilantro,
  finely chopped

1¼ cups sour cream

handful of grated Cheddar

This has chipotle chillies—dried and smoked jalapeños—at its heart. They have a wonderful rich depth and really make the stew. You can get them and the Mexican oregano through the Internet.

Preheat the oven to 300°F.

Heat the oil in a large flameproof cast-iron or enamelled casserole and brown the meat over a high heat, in batches. Scoop out of the pot and set aside. Reduce the heat to medium. Add the onions and garlic to the pot and soften for about 10 minutes.

Return the meat to the pot, add the passata, vinegar, chipotles, bay leaves, oregano, and a big pinch of salt. Bring to a boil, then cover and cook in the oven for 3 hours, or until the meat is meltingly tender.

Serve with fresh tortillas, chopped cilantro, sour cream, and grated Cheddar.

Sambutes

{ MAKES 25–30 }

olive oil, for frying

1 onion, finely chopped

1 habanero or Scotch bonnet
   chilli, finely chopped

½ pound ground pork

several soft corn tortillas

⅓ cup plus 1½ teaspoons
   all-purpose flour, mixed with
   water to make a paste

1¼ cups sour cream,
   to serve

salsa, to serve (see pages 226–7)

This is a take on *salbutes*, a classic dish from Mexico's
Yucatán Peninsula. Deep-fried filled tortillas, stuffed with a
spicy pork mix. This is habanero land—big fruit, mega kick.

Heat a little olive oil in a large, heavy-based frying pan
and soften the onion and chilli over a medium–high heat.
Add the pork and cook for 4–5 minutes, stirring frequently,
until lightly browned.

Using a 2-inch cookie cutter cut 50–60 small circles from
the tortillas.

Put 1 heaped teaspoon of the pork mixture onto a tortilla
circle, then top with another tortilla circle, using the flour
paste to seal the edges and pinching them together.

Heat 2 inches of oil in a wide, heavy-based pan over
medium–high heat and fry the *sambutes* in batches for
2–3 minutes, turning once, until golden brown and cooked
through. Drain on paper towels.

Serve the hot *sambutes* with the sour cream and salsa if you
like.

Cochinita pibil

{ SERVES 8 }

2 tablespoons cumin seeds

1 tablespoon juniper berries

10 whole cloves

3 ounces *recado de achiote*
   paste

generous 2 cups Seville orange
   juice (or, if out of season,
   1⅔ cups freshly squeezed
   orange juice and ½ cup
   lemon juice)

sea salt

1 large pork shoulder, boned,
   cut into large cubes

1 packet of banana leaves
   (optional)

cooked tortillas, to serve

salsa, to serve (see pages 226–7)

A classic dish from the Yucatán region of Mexico, transforming a shoulder of pork into meltingly tender strands of piggy bliss. It's traditionally cooked in the *pib*, a pit lined with hot stones. The meat is wrapped in banana leaves, dropped onto the searing stones, then covered with wet sacking, followed by more hot rocks and embers, then a final topping of earth to fill the pit. This could prove impractical in the average kitchen, so a slow oven is fine. *Achiote* paste (made from the small red seeds of the annatto tree) gives the all-important red colour and a good depth of flavour. Seville orange juice is best for the marinade, but the oranges have only a short winter season. Fresh orange juice (not that horrible concentrated stuff) mixed with a little lemon is a good substitute.

Grind the cumin, juniper berries, and cloves in a coffee grinder. Blend the spice mix, *achiote* paste, and orange juice in a food processor. Season with salt, to taste.

Marinate the cubes of pork shoulder in the spiced orange juice, covered, in the fridge for at least 12 hours.

Preheat the oven to 325°F.

Wash the banana leaves, if using, and quickly pass them over a burner to soften them or blanch them in a pan of boiling water. Line a roasting pan with the banana leaves, making sure that you'll be able to fold them over the pork once you place it in the pan. (If you can't get banana leaves, cook the pork in a covered casserole or a dish tightly covered with a double thickness of foil.) Add the pork and the marinade, cover with foil, and cook in the oven for about 4–4½ hours, until tender. Ideally, leave it to cool, then put it in the fridge, covered, overnight. The next day, reheat thoroughly, adding a touch of oil.

An hour before you are going to eat the pork, make the chilli-pickled onion. Rinse the red onion in a strainer under cold running water for a couple of minutes; set aside to dry. Place the chilli in a bowl with the onion and cover with the cider vinegar. To serve, remove the onion from the vinegar.

When the pork is ready, use a fork to shred the meat, removing big chunks of fat. Serve with the juices, fresh tortillas, and salsa.

For chilli-pickled red onions
1 red onion, thinly sliced
1 Scotch bonnet or habanero
   chilli, very thinly sliced
3 tablespoons cider vinegar

Guacamole

5 ripe avocados

2 red onions, finely chopped

2 jalapeño or finger chillies,
    finely chopped

4 ripe tomatoes, peeled,
    seeded, and finely chopped

juice of 2 limes

sea salt and freshly ground
    black pepper

Real guacamole is a riot of textures, and manages to combine the creamy, sharp, and spicy. The real thing is miles removed from that snot-green wallpaper paste that plays host to more chemicals than an ICI plant. The avocados must be ripe, so you can mash them with a fork—never use a food processor; I do like the odd chunk left in. Everyone's tastes are different, so feel free to increase onions and cut down on chillies and the rest.

Peel and pit the avocados and mash them roughly, using a large fork. Add the onions, chillies, tomatoes, and lime juice. Season to taste and serve.

Mole verde

A *mole* is far more than mere sauce. "The King of Mexican cuisine," writes Patricia Quintana in *The Taste of Mexico* (Stewart, Tabori & Chang, 1986). It's a true Mexican *mélange*, available in a thousand different variations. One of the richest, and certainly the most famous, is the *mole poblano* from Puebla: it melds anise, clove, cinnamon, black peppers, and chillies with garlic, tomatillos, sesame seeds, ground almonds, peanuts, and bitter chocolate. A complex and time-consuming dish, sure, but magnificent, too. This is a green version, thickened with toasted pumpkin seeds and made verdant with cilantro, tomatillo, and lettuce. It's rich and comforting, with a slight chilli kick.

Put 1½ quarts water in a saucepan, add the onion, bay leaf, and a pinch of salt, and bring to a boil. Add the chicken pieces, ensuring they are fully immersed, skim off any scum, put a lid on, and simmer gently for about 45 minutes, or until cooked through. Let the chicken cool in the broth, then remove it and set it aside. Strain the broth into a bowl and skim off the fat with kitchen paper towels.

To make the sauce, heat a frying pan over a medium heat for 5 minutes, then pour in the pumpkin seeds in a single layer. When the first seed pops, cook and stir for up to 5 minutes, until all have popped. Leave to cool. Grind in a food processor or spice grinder, then stir into scant 1 cup of the chicken cooking broth.

{ CONTINUES OVERLEAF }

{ SERVES 4 }

1 onion, finely chopped

1 bay leaf

sea salt

1 (4-pound) chicken (the best you can afford), cut in half, then in half again

boiled rice, to serve

For the sauce

¾ cup pumpkin seeds

2 (13-ounce) cans tomatillos, or use homegrown green tomatoes or 1 (28-ounce) can chopped tomatoes, drained

4 fresh jalapeño chillies (or from a jar in brine, drained), finely chopped

6 large romaine lettuce leaves

½ onion, roughly chopped

4 garlic cloves, roughly chopped

2 cups cilantro, plus a handful to garnish

½ teaspoon cumin seeds

6 whole black peppercorns

1 (¾-inch) piece of cinnamon stick

3–4 cloves

1 tablespoon lard or vegetable oil

sea salt

Put the tomatillos and chillies into a blender. Tear the lettuce leaves and add to the blender, along with the onion, garlic, and cilantro. Grind the cumin, peppercorns, cinnamon, and cloves in a spice grinder or with a pestle and mortar, then add to the blender and blitz until smooth.

Heat the lard or oil in a large saucepan and, when hot, add the pumpkin seed mixture and cook, stirring, until it thickens and darkens, about 5 minutes. Add the tomatillo and spice blend and cook, stirring for a few more minutes, until darker still.

Add 1¾ cups of the broth, reduce the heat to medium–low, and simmer, partially covered, for about 30 minutes.

Shred the chicken, removing the skin, and add to the simmering sauce. Cook to heat through for 10 minutes. Serve with rice.

A trio of ceviches

Ceviche. One word guaranteed to pique the taste buds. Freshness of the fish is paramount, as you're serving it pretty much raw, save a light "cooking" in acidic citrus juice. It should dance off the tongue, gloriously pert, refreshing, and zingy.

Any country with a coastline in South and Central America will claim credit and each will proclaim theirs the best. In truth, the dish probably had Polynesian root, although anywhere with an abundant supply of fresh fish and acidic medium (citrus juice, vinegar) would have used this technique. In the Philippines I tried a dish called *kinilaw*, where raw fish is simply dipped in vinegar. Very good it was, too, and could even be the daddy of them all.

The fish needs no more than 30 minutes in the citrus juice—any longer and you obliterate the piscine sweetness with an acidic hammer. Chilli adds essential heat, red onions crunch and bite, tomatoes soft sweetness. Pomegranate seeds add tiny, refreshing bursts of intense pink, too.

Use any white fish you like, but I tend to use bream. It's not too expensive and has good texture and flavour. Get the fishmonger to fillet, skin, and pin-bone your fish. Cod's good, too, as are sea bass and haddock. If you can buy it fresh enough, even pollack's just about acceptable.

Avocado prawns, ceviche-style

I far prefer those small, pink, comma-like North Atlantic prawns to the bland tiger prawns, often farmed in the East to ruinous environmental effect. If you can, buy them whole and peel. Every supermarket has them and even the cooked ones are OK. If you can find fresh ones, then all the better.

Put the prawns in a bowl with the lime juice, Tabasco, and a big pinch of salt and pepper. Cover and leave in the fridge for 30 minutes. Mix in the onions, chillies, and cilantro. Serve in halved avocados. (Alternatively, mash the avocados, mix with the prawn ceviche, and serve atop tortillas or stuffed into pitta bread).

{ SERVES 4 }

1 pound small cooked Atlantic
  prawns, peeled (or fresh,
  uncooked prawns)
juice of 1 lime
few drops of Tabasco sauce
sea salt and freshly ground
  black pepper
2 red onions, finely chopped
6 bird's-eye chillies, finely
  chopped (or ½ habanero chilli
  if you want real heat, or a
  couple of standard green
  chillies if you really can't face
  heat, finely chopped)
small bunch of cilantro,
  finely chopped
4 avocados

Bells of St. Clement's ceviche

Seville orange juice, mixed 50:50 with lemon juice, gives a bittersweet edge to this dish, accentuated by ruby shards of pomegranate seeds. Substitute normal orange juice with a good splash of grapefruit juice for the Seville juice when Seville's out of season. Which is most of the year.

Slice the fish in ½-inch-wide strips, then cut into dice. Place in a bowl and mix with the orange and lemon juices. Cover and leave in the fridge for 30 minutes, or until the fish is completely white and opaque.

Cut the pomegranate in half, hold over a plate, then whack the uncut side of each half with a rolling pin until the seeds drop out. Discard the white pith.

Mix the marinated fish with the pomegranate seeds, chillies, red onion, cilantro, and a big pinch of salt. Serve with tortilla chips.

{ SERVES 4 }

1 (2¼-pound) bass, filleted, skinned, and pin-bones removed

juice of 2 Seville oranges (or 1 normal orange and ½ grapefruit)

juice of 1 lemon

1 ripe pomegranate

3 green finger chillies, or 3 jalapeños, or 1 Scotch bonnet, finely chopped

1 red onion, finely chopped

big handful of cilantro, roughly chopped

sea salt

tortilla chips, to serve

Classic ceviche

{ SERVES 4 }

1 (2¼-pound) bream, filleted,
skinned, and pin-bones
removed

juice of 2 limes

3 tomatoes, peeled, seeded,
and finely diced

3 jalapeño chillies or
1 habanero, finely chopped
(the latter is far hotter, but
does have the most wonderful
fruity depth)

1 red onion, finely chopped

big handful of cilantro, finely
chopped, plus extra sprigs to
garnish

sea salt

4 soft tortillas, fried until crisp,
to serve (optional)

1 avocado, cut in half and sliced
lengthwise, to serve

Slice the fish into ½-inch-wide strips, then cut into dice.
Put in a bowl, mix with the lime juice, and leave in the
fridge, covered, for 30 minutes, or until the fish is
completely white and opaque.

Gently mix in the diced tomatoes, chillies, onion, cilantro,
and a big pinch of sea salt.

Serve (on fried tortillas, if you like) with slices of avocado
and sprigs of cilantro.

A trio of salsas

{ EACH RECIPE MAKES
  A BOWL FOR 6–8 }

No Mexican feast is complete without salsas, ranging from the fresh to the smoky to the fairly hot. You can then customize the taco to your own tastes.

Salsa pico de gallo

{ SERVES 6–8 }

2 white onions, finely chopped
5 tomatoes, peeled, seeded,
  and finely chopped
4 serrano chillies, finely
  chopped (or thin finger chillies
  if serranos are not available)
juice of 1 lime
sea salt
big handful of cilantro,
  roughly chopped

The classic, crunchy all-purpose salsa, this is never far from the Mexican table. It's refreshing, too, perfect for cutting through some of the fattier local favourites.

Mix the onions, tomatoes, chillies, and lime juice in a bowl; add salt to taste. Leave for an hour, add the cilantro, then serve.

A roasted, fiery salsa

The habanero chilli is the main player here, so this is hot. But the roasted tomatoes add depth and a proper smoky tang.

Preheat the oven to 400°F. Put the tomatoes on a baking sheet, sprinkle with salt and pepper and a splash of olive oil. Roast until the edges char and the tomatoes are soft, about 25 minutes.

Put the tomatoes in a blender, with the chillies, vinegar, and a big pinch of salt. Blend until smooth.

{ SERVES 6–8 }

8 tomatoes, halved
sea salt and freshly ground
  black pepper
a splash of olive oil
4–12 habanero or Scotch bonnet
  chillies, stalks removed
3 tablespoons white
  wine vinegar

A warm, smoky salsa

Heat and smoke. This is all about the chipotle, the smoked and dried jalapeño chilli.

Heat the oil in a saucepan over a medium heat. Add the onion and garlic and soften for about 10 minutes, then add the chillies and cook for 2 minutes.

Add the tomatoes, vinegar, oregano, sugar, and salt and pepper to taste and simmer gently for 20 minutes. Set aside to cool before serving.

{ SERVES 6–8 }

2 tablespoons peanut oil
1 onion, finely chopped
2 garlic cloves, finely chopped
3–6 dried chipotle chillies,
  soaked in water for 15 minutes,
  drained, and finely chopped
3 large tomatoes, peeled, seeded,
  and finely chopped
2 tablespoons white wine
  vinegar
pinch of dried oregano
pinch of superfine sugar
sea salt and freshly ground
  black pepper

{ Sichuan food }

Ma. Nope not some shrugging gesture of "whatever." Nor the smacking of lips. Rather the Sichuan term for "numbing," a reaction caused by Sichuan peppers. They're small, red, and dried, and have a wonderfully fragrant citrus tang. But when mixed with dried chillies, the effect becomes "hot and numbing," perhaps the most famous facet of this regional Chinese cuisine.

Once upon a time, not so many years back, the UK was in thrall to Cantonese cooking. After all, most immigrants came from Hong Kong and southern China. And so we believed Chinese food was all about dim sum, delicate (or not-so-delicate) steamed fish, and sweet-and-sour pork, unaware of the eight distinct culinary regions of that vast land.

Slowly, though, we're beginning to appreciate the various regions, as new restaurants open up. But it was Fuchsia Dunlop's brilliant *Sichuan Cookery* (Penguin, 2001) that really got things going over here.

She was the first Westerner to learn to cook at the Sichuan Institute of Higher Cuisine in Chengdu. She taught us about a fascinating cuisine with 23 different flavour combinations, not all hot or numbing. "Fish fragrant" is a fish-free combination of sweet, salty, sour, and spicy. "Scorched chilli" is best seen in a cucumber salad that manages to heat the tongue and cool the mouth simultaneously.

"China is the place for food," goes the old saying, "but Sichuan the place for flavour."

Gong bao chicken

This Sichuan dish is better known, in the States at least, as *kung pao* chicken. But the versions I've tried are pretty drab, relying on peanuts and peppers rather than the elegant balance of ingredients that characterizes the original. The key is to chop the chicken into similar-size small cubes, so it cooks quickly and evenly.

Mix all the marinade ingredients in a bowl with 1 tablespoon water. Add the chicken, cover, and leave to marinate in the fridge for 2 hours.

Make the sauce by mixing all the ingredients in a bowl or other container. Set aside.

When you are ready to cook the chicken, heat the peanut oil in a wok until it is very hot but not smoking. Add the chillies and Sichuan peppercorns and stir-fry until crisp and fragrant, but don't let them burn.

Lift the chicken out of the marinade with a slotted spoon, add it to the wok, and stir-fry over a high heat. Add a little marinade if it is too dry.

Once the chicken has turned white and firmed up, 2–3 minutes, add the scallions, ginger, and garlic, and stir-fry for 2 minutes more; make sure the chicken is cooked through.

Add the sauce, stirring all the time. Once everything is thick and shiny, add the cashew nuts and serve with steamed rice.

{ SERVES 2 }

1⅓ pounds chicken breast, cut into small cubes
2 tablespoons peanut oil
6–30 Sichuan dried chillies
1½ tablespoons whole Sichuan peppercorns
7 scallions, white parts only, cut on a diagonal
1 (2-inch) piece of fresh ginger, thinly sliced using a vegetable peeler
4 garlic cloves, thinly sliced
2½ ounces cashew nuts
steamed rice, to serve

For the marinade
5 teaspoons light soy sauce
2 teaspoons dark soy sauce
2 teaspoons Shaoxing rice wine
1½ teaspoons potato flour

For the sauce
2 teaspoons rice vinegar
3 tablespoons chicken stock
1 teaspoon superfine sugar
1½ teaspoons potato flour
2 teaspoons light soy sauce
2 teaspoons dark soy sauce
6 teaspoons black Chinese vinegar
3 teaspoons sesame oil

Dan dan noodles

I first ate these not on the spice-scented streets of Chengdu, but in the rather less exotic environs of London's Soho. Barshu might not have been the first Sichuan restaurant to open in the capital but it is certainly the best. Sichuan's famed "hot and numbing" flavour is based on chilli and the wonderfully citrus Sichuan pepper. This is a classic Sichuan street snack. If you can't find the preserved vegetables, don't worry.

Heat the oil in a wok over a medium heat. When it is hot but not smoking, add the chillies and Sichuan peppercorns and stir-fry briefly until the oil is fragrant. Take care not to burn the spices.

Add the *ya cai* or preserved vegetable and continue to stir-fry until hot and fragrant. Add the ground beef, splash in the soy sauce, and stir-fry until the meat is brown and a little crisp, but not too dry. When the meat is cooked, remove the wok from the heat and set aside.

To make the sauce, combine the ingredients, divide between 2 serving bowls, and mix well.

Cook the noodles according to the instructions on the package. Drain them and add a portion to the sauce in each serving bowl. Sprinkle each bowl with the meat mixture and give the noodles a good stir until the sauce and meat are evenly distributed. Serve garnished with scallions.

{ SERVES 2 }

1 tablespoon peanut oil
3 Sichuan dried chillies, snipped
    in half, seeds discarded
½ teaspoon whole Sichuan
    peppercorns
1 ounce Sichuan *ya cai* or
    tianjin preserved vegetable,
    thinly sliced
¼ pound ground beef
2 teaspoons light soy sauce
10½ ounces dried Chinese
    noodles
scallions, green part only, cut
    into thin rounds, to garnish

For the sauce
½–1 teaspoon ground roasted
    Sichuan peppercorns
1 tablespoon light soy sauce
1 tablespoon dark soy sauce
2 tablespoons chilli oil, with
    chilli sediment

Chicken chanko

{ SERVES 4 }

1 (4-pound) chicken, boned,
  bones reserved, meat cut into
  1-inch chunks
4 large carrots
3 large leeks
2 large onions
8 whole peppercorns
½ cup soy sauce
½ daikon (white radish or mooli)
½ Chinese cabbage
½ cup sake
12 fresh shiitake mushrooms
14 ounces fresh firm tofu,
  drained and diced, cut into
  1-inch cubes
sea salt
1⅓ pounds fresh
  udon noodles

People tend to see Japanese food as endlessly light and elegant, all sushi, sashimi, and artfully carved fruit. But this is just one part of the cuisine. Because Japan can get mighty cold in winter (except in the tropical south), so good, belly lining tucker is desired. Think of *tonkatsu*, or breaded pork chop. And the sweetish curry rice, along with the ever-popular *ramen* (actually Chinese in origin), the ultimate in booze food. *Chankonabe*, better known as *chanko*, is a great filler, a chuck-it-all-in casserole devoured by sumo wrestlers, those great wobbling man-mountains. It's a communal, one-pot dish with simmering stock, into which is dipped chicken, pork, mushrooms, potatoes, carrots, onions, lotus root, and pretty much anything else around. They're cooked and eaten, and the remaining stock is then drunk with rice and noodles. It's pretty hefty, but contains a minimal amount of fat. One particularly mighty sumo, Takamisugi, devoured 65 bowls in one sitting. He only stopped when his jaw began to hurt. "If you wanna be a *rikishi* (sumo)," says the legendary Konishiki, "you've gotta eat *chanko*." And even if you don't harbor ambitions of slapping a multi-bellied beast from the chalk circle, it still makes for a good feasting dish.

Put the chicken bones in a large pot along with 1 quartered carrot, 1 quartered leek, 1 quartered onion, the peppercorns, and the soy sauce. Cover with water, bring to a boil, skim, then simmer on a very low heat for 3 hours. Strain the

{ CONTINUES OVERLEAF }

stock into a large clean pan, skim again. Place the pan of stock over the heat and bring to a simmer.

Cut the remaining carrots and leeks into ¼-inch slices; cut the remaining onion in half, then slice thickly; cut the daikon into cubes. Blanch these vegetables for 2 minutes in the simmering stock, then remove with a slotted spoon and set aside.

Take 6 leaves of Chinese cabbage, blanch in the stock for 10 seconds, then remove, roll up the leaves, and cut crosswise into ¼-inch strips.

Add the chicken to the stock and simmer for 8–10 minutes. Return the leek and onion to the stock and cook for another minute. Add the carrots, daikon, and sake and cook for 1 minute more, or until the chicken is cooked through.

Finally, add the mushrooms, tofu, and cabbage and cook for 1 minute. Using a slotted spoon, scoop all the ingredients out of the stock into 4 bowls. Add the noodles to the stock and boil for a few minutes, until just tender. Ladle the noodles and broth into the bowls. Eat, then lie down for a few hours, moaning softly.

Japanese aubergine

I could never get too excited about the aubergine. Interested, yes, but thrilled, no. That is, until I tried a dish at Roka—one of the best contemporary Japanese restaurants in London—that made the taste buds swoon. It turns the aubergine into something soft, silken, and wonderfully savoury.

Preheat the oven to 350°F.

Halve the aubergine lengthwise and slash the flesh, not too deeply, in a crisscross pattern. Place on a baking sheet, brush with vegetable oil, and season with salt, then bake for 15–20 minutes, turning over after 8 minutes, until golden but just firm.

Meanwhile, in a small pan, mix the white and red misos with the sugar, sake, mirin, and soy sauce. Heat gently, stirring, until the sugar has dissolved and the liquid has reduced and thickened. Preheat the broiler to high.

Remove the aubergine from the oven and paint the miso mixture all over the flesh side. Broil until the surface is scattered with black and golden spots.

{ SERVES 2 }

1 long Asian aubergine
  (a normal one is fine, too)
1 teaspoon vegetable oil
sea salt
2 tablespoons sweet white miso
1 tablespoon red miso
1 teaspoon superfine sugar
2 tablespoons sake
2 tablespoons mirin
1 teaspoon soy sauce

Asian-style bass, John Dory, or other big white fish

This is a fusion dish of sorts, mixing wine and olive oil with soy sauce and rice vinegar. But it does work. You can use any white fish in this recipe, and either a whole fish, or fillets. As the flavours are strong, farmed bass is fine, though nowhere near wild bass. John Dory has exceptional sweetness, but it's best to buy it filleted, as there's a lot of bone.

If you have a whole fish, make 3 shallow diagonal cuts along one side of it using a sharp knife. Put it on a big piece of foil on a baking sheet, season it inside and out, and fill the belly with the lemon, garlic, and chilli. (If using fillets, arrange them on a big piece of foil on a baking sheet, season, and cover with the lemon, garlic, and chilli.)

For the marinade, mix all the ingredients together. Pour the marinade over the fish, cover, and place in the fridge for an hour, turning once.

Preheat the oven to 400°F.

Fold the edges of the foil up to make a dish, then pour over the wine. Bake for 20–25 minutes, 10 minutes less for fillets. Test if the fish is cooked before serving; it should flake easily when pressed with a knife.

{ SERVES 4}

1 (2¾-pound) bass, scaled and gutted, or the fillets from 2 John Dory
sea salt and freshly ground black pepper
1 lemon, sliced
1 garlic clove, thinly sliced
1 habanero chilli, thinly sliced (optional)
½ cup dry white wine

For the marinade
2 tablespoons light soy sauce
1 tablespoon dry white wine
2 tablespoons olive oil
1 teaspoon rice wine vinegar

Sisig (Filipino pork)

{ SERVES 6 }

1 (2¼-pound) pork belly (or
  1 2¼ pounds boned pig's head
  meat: jowls, ears, and cheek),
  cut into ½-inch cubes
2⅛ cups pineapple juice
1 tablespoon sea salt
1 tablespoon whole black
  peppercorns
6 chicken livers
2 large white onions,
  finely chopped
2 tablespoons lime juice, plus
  lime wedges to serve
¼ cup white vinegar
6–20 bird's-eye chillies, plus
  extra to serve
freshly ground black pepper

Filipino food is one of Asia's great hidden secrets. We "go out" for a Thai green chicken curry, "slurp" a Vietnamese *pho,* and "murder" a Chinese feast. Yet what about the food of the Philippines, a country that looks both east and west (thanks to over half a century of occupation by the Spanish and then Americans)? It's not as vivid and spicy as most Thai food, nor as delicate as Vietnamese. Vinegar is of huge importance, and many dishes tend towards the sweet. But I had a blast in Manila, an underloved and overlooked city. Sure, it ain't no looker. Dirty, chaotic, and smog-filled. But it's got heart and soul and charm. This is a classic booze dish, and should use the whole of a pig's head. But I've adapted it to use pork belly. It's all about the contrast of textures: crisp, soft, and crunchy. The citrus juice hews through the fat, the chillies add heat. It's one of the world's great dishes, and I ate endless versions. If you have a good butcher, ask him for a pig's head. Scorch off the hairs, then poach and bone it so you're left with the ears, snout, and all that wonderful cheek meat. I've adapted this recipe from one in *Kulinarya* (Avon Publishing, 2008), a great guide to Philippine cuisine.

Put the pork belly (or head meat), pineapple juice, salt, and peppercorns in a stockpot with 2 quarts water. Cover and bring to the boil, then reduce to a simmer and cook for 1 hour.

{ CONTINUES OVERLEAF }

Heat a barbecue so the coals are glowing white-hot.

After 1 hour cooking, add the chicken livers to the pork and cook for 15 minutes more until the meat is fork-tender. Remove the pork and chicken livers from the pot and discard the liquid. Grill the pork over the hot charcoal, or fry over a high heat in a heavy-based pan, until the skin is brown and crisp.

Chop the chicken livers into small cubes, mix with the pork, and place in a bowl. Mix in the onions, lime juice, vinegar, and chillies. Season to taste with salt and pepper.

Heat a cast-iron griddle pan until white hot, then add the meat mixture. Cook for 3–5 minutes. This is the third cooking stage, where the meat becomes browner and crunchier still.

Serve sizzling hot, with cold beer and extra chillies and lime wedges on the side.

Filipino beef stew (Adobong baka)

They say that *adobo* is the Filipino national dish. There are hundreds of versions, but it's actually a technique, meaning anything cooked in vinegar. I spent a week in and around Manila and two meals stand out. The first, in Pampanga, just north of the city, was with artist, chef, and all-round Renaissance man Claude Tayag. He showed me that Filipino food was far more than the brown, greasy stereotype perpetuated across the world. We ate this *adobo* and *sinigang*: a sour, clear soup with seafood and all manner of other things. The second was dinner with the beautiful Margarita Fores and friends. There, we devoured some of the finest *lechon* (roasted suckling pig) I've tasted, with skin as thin and brittle as glazed caramel. Incredible.

In a large bowl, combine the garlic, peppercorns, vinegar, soy sauce, and bay leaves. Add the beef, cover, and marinate in the fridge for at least an hour; 6 hours would be better.

Preheat the oven to 300°F.

Remove the meat from the marinade. Heat 2 tablespoons of the oil in an ovenproof pan and brown the meat in batches over a high heat, adding extra oil as needed. Transfer to a plate and set aside. Add the marinade to the pan with 2 cups water. Bring to the boil, then reduce to a simmer and add the beef, topping up with a little extra water, if needed, so the ribs are just covered.

Put the pan in the oven and cook for 2–2½ hours, or until the meat is fork-tender. Season with salt to taste. Serve with rice and cold beer.

{ SERVES 6 }

6 garlic cloves, finely chopped
½ teaspoon whole black peppercorns, crushed
½ cup cane, palm, or white wine vinegar
4 tablespoons soy sauce
2 bay leaves
2¼ pounds beef short ribs or brisket, boned and cut into 2-inch cubes
4 tablespoons peanut oil
sea salt
boiled white rice, to serve

Goan mutton vindaloo

{ SERVES 6 }

6 whole cloves

1 (2-inch) piece of
cinnamon stick

10 whole peppercorns

½ star anise

1 teaspoon cumin seeds

1 teaspoon poppy seeds

15–20 dried red Kashmiri
chillies, soaked in cold water
for 15 minutes, drained

6 plump garlic cloves,
finely chopped

1 (1-inch) piece of fresh
ginger, finely chopped

4 teaspoons cider vinegar

1 tablespoon tamarind pulp

1¾ pounds mutton (wether), cut
into big chunks

¼ cup vegetable oil

3 onions, finely chopped

sea salt

½ teaspoon jaggery (or palm
sugar), or to taste

15 curry leaves

handful of cilantro, finely
chopped

boiled basmati rice, to serve

Ah, vindaloo, that ultimate test of pungency prowess, a curry so fierce that it batters its way through the fizzy fug of a twelve-pint night. Nice. The curry house version is about extreme, one-note heat; forget delicate spicing and subtle technique, this is basically a Madras (itself an English Indian invention) with an extra dose of chilli powder. I have to admit a fondness for this culinary bovver boy, but once you've tasted the real thing, there's no going back.

Vindaloo comes from Goa, the small coastal Indian state colonized by the Portuguese a few centuries back. Along with the English and Spanish, they were great seafarers and Empire builders, and actually introduced chillies to India. Mix this ingredient with pork preserved in vinegar and garlic (so it could last the long journey out at sea) and you have the basis for the dish. Vindaloo fuses the Portuguese word for wine (and by extension vinegar), *vin*, with *alhos*, or garlic. And as Goa was Christian, pork was permitted, while it was taboo in the rest of India. In time, the Portuguese wine vinegar was replaced with toddy, or the local palm vinegar. My version substitutes mutton for pork, but is equally good. Don't be put off by the long list of ingredients. You should have most of them anyway, and the actual cooking is very easy indeed.

Put the cloves, cinnamon, peppercorns, star anise, cumin, and poppy seeds in a dry, heavy-based pan and roast over low to medium heat for a few minutes, until fragrant. Leave to cool, then grind using a pestle and mortar or an electric spice grinder.

Put the chillies, garlic, ginger, vinegar, and tamarind
into a blender and blitz until you have a smooth paste.
Add the ground dry spices and blitz for a few seconds.

Use one-fifth of the spice paste to coat the mutton; cover
and refrigerate for 30 minutes.

Meanwhile, heat the oil in a large enamelled casserole and
fry the onions for 15–20 minutes, or until brown. Add the
remaining spice paste and fry for 5 minutes more, stirring
continuously. Add a couple of tablespoons of water if the
mixture starts to dry out.

Preheat the oven to 275°F.

Add the mutton to the pan and fry in the spice mixture
for 5 minutes. Add 3⅓ cups water, and season
to taste with salt and jaggery. Cook in the oven for about
2½ hours, or until tender.

Stir in the curry leaves and simmer for 3–4 minutes. Then
mix in the cilantro and serve with basmati rice.

Rogan josh

{ SERVES 4 }

2 pounds mutton chops
  (and 1 pound mutton bones, if
  you can get them)
2 teaspoons sea salt
5 ounces Greek yogurt
1 tablespoon Kashmiri
  chilli powder
1 tablespoon paprika
4 tablespoons sunflower oil
1 pound shallots,
  finely chopped
6 garlic cloves, finely chopped
8 whole cloves
6 green cardamom pods,
  crushed
2 black cardamom pods, crushed
2 teaspoons fennel powder
large pinch of saffron strands
1 teaspoon grated nutmeg
1 teaspoon ground coriander
1 teaspoon ground ginger
4 bay leaves
small handful of cilantro,
  roughly chopped, to serve
boiled basmati rice, to serve

This is a recipe from my friend Bill, a man whose love for India matches mine for Mexico and Thailand. I've travelled the globe with him on many occasions, and he's a trencherman in the truest form. Anyway, his take on the classic Kashmiri dish is wonderful. When buying mutton, ask for a wether (adolescent sheep) rather than an old boiler. The flavour is there but not overwhelming.

Put the chops and bones in a big saucepan, cover with 7 cups water, add the salt, put the lid on, and bring to the boil. Simmer for 30 minutes, then remove the chops, cover, and put in the fridge. Discard the bones and skim off the scum from the liquid. Boil the stock over a high heat to reduce by half, 20–30 minutes, and reserve.

Meanwhile, put the yogurt in a small bowl, add the chilli powder and paprika and whisk together; cover and set aside.

Heat 2 tablespoons of the oil in a frying pan and fry the shallots over a low heat for 15 minutes until nearly caramelized. Add the garlic, cloves, and cardamom pods and fry for 2 minutes more. Remove from the heat and add the rest of the spices (but not the bay leaves). Stir in 2 tablespoons of the stock, then blitz to a paste in a blender or food processor.

Heat the rest of the oil in an enamelled casserole, then fry the chops over a medium–high heat for 2–3 minutes on each side, or until browned. Add the shallot paste, yogurt mixture, bay leaves, and half the stock, bring gently to a simmer, cover, and cook on a very low heat until the meat is tender, about 2 hours. Top up with stock if it becomes dry. Taste and add more salt if necessary. Serve, sprinkled with cilantro, with basmati rice.

Yellow dhal

**{ SERVES 4 WITH
OTHER DISHES }**

8 ounce mung dhal (yellow split
  mung beans)
2 green chillies,
  roughly chopped
1 red chilli, roughly chopped
1 (¾-inch) piece of fresh ginger,
  finely chopped
2 fresh or canned tomatoes,
  roughly chopped
1 teaspoon cumin seeds,
  lightly toasted
3 whole cloves, crumbled
pinch of turmeric
2 teaspoons sea salt
4 garlic cloves, finely sliced
12 curry leaves
handful of fresh cilantro,
  roughly chopped
3 scallions, finely sliced
1 tablespoon sunflower oil

Indian comfort food at its best. You'll find this all over the
north and central regions of the country. I remember having
a version in a truck stop in Madhur Pradesh. As burly
truckers snoozed on tattered *charpoys*, we dug in. I was
expecting creamy comfort and got a dish so hot it nuked the
roof of my mouth. But who says lentils are boring? They're
far too good to leave for the hippies to muck up. A poached
egg sat on top makes for a very civilized lunch.

Soak the mung dhal in water for 30 minutes, then drain
and rinse. In a big saucepan, bring 5 cups of water to a boil.
Add the mung dhal, chillies, ginger, tomatoes, cumin,
cloves, turmeric, salt, and half of the garlic. Bring to a boil,
then boil for 10 minutes. Reduce the heat and simmer for
40 minutes more until the mung dhal soften and the
mixture becomes almost soupy.

Using a stick blender or an egg whisk, beat until the dhal
have mostly broken up keep a nubbly texture. Add the
curry leaves, cilantro, and scallions, then return to the heat
for a couple of minutes. Remove from the heat and taste,
adding more salt if necessary.

Heat the oil in a small frying pan and fry the rest of the
garlic until light brown. Pour over the dhal, and serve.

Steamed fish, Cantonese-style

The Cantonese are obsessed with the freshest of fish. Hence those vast aquariums with gloomy-looking sea life, ready to be fished out to order. This is a simple dish, so much depends on the quality of the fish. You can use a dedicated fish steamer, a large bamboo basket, or even a colander inside a wok (make sure the bottom of the colander doesn't touch the water).

Rinse and dry the fish, inside and out. Make 3 shallow diagonal cuts into each side of it and rub with salt. Rub a little into the cavity, too. Put the fish on a heatproof platter and scatter with the ginger.

Fill the steamer or wok with about 2 inches of water and bring to a boil. Put the fish platter into the steamer or wok, cover and steam for 20 minutes or more, depending on the size of the fish. The fish should be opaque, and flake easily away from the bone.

Remove the fish platter and pour off any excess liquid, then pour over the soy sauces.

In a small pan, heat both oils together until they begin to shimmer, then pour over the fish and top with scallions. Serve with steamed rice.

{ SERVES 2 }

1 (1–2¼-pound), very fresh, firm-fleshed white fish, such as bass, sole, or snapper, gutted and scaled but head on
big pinch of salt
1 (2-inch) piece of fresh ginger, cut into long shreds
3 tablespoons light soy sauce
1 tablespoon dark soy sauce
2 teaspoons sesame oil
1 tablespoon peanut oil
5 scallions, shredded
steamed rice, to serve

{ Cooking for children }

I'm not a nutritionist or dietitian. Thank God, because the vast majority talk crap. There are good ones, though, sensible and pragmatic. Once my daughter Lola moved onto solid food, at around five months, I panicked. I couldn't use salt, or spice, or chilli, the basis of most things I cook. But I took recipes from Annabel Karmel (someone I do rate) and Mark Hix's *Eat Up: Food for Children of All Ages* (Fourth Estate, 2003) and adapted them as time went on.

For me, fresh food is always best. You don't want any salt in the first year or so—and keep it low after that. But anything is better than those dreary ready-made pots. However posh or organic or free-range they profess to be, they all taste exactly the same: oversweet and deathly dull.

I've never cooked anything I wouldn't eat myself for my children. Not that I'd want to exist solely on apple purée or chicken and carrots. All these recipes have proper flavour.

I tended to make big batches of dishes once a week, then freeze them in small pots. A stick blender was an essential accessory (for the first year, mush is order of the day) and a steamer, too. Both my children can be fussy, and usually prefer a bag of chips or package of Haribo to a lovingly prepared lunch. There's nothing wrong with treats. It's only when junk becomes the mainstay of a child's diet that things go wrong. Mine both go through stages: one loving pasta and tomato sauce, the other hating it. I try not to force food on my children, but, on the other hand, they play us like pros. Balance, pragmatism, and patience are key.

Big beefy stew

3 tablespoons unsalted butter

2 tablespoons olive oil

1 pound braising or chuck steak,
   fat removed, cut into
   1½-inch cubes

3 small onions, finely chopped

6 carrots, finely chopped

¾ pound sweet potatoes, peeled
   and cut into 1½-inch cubes

9 ounces button
   mushrooms, sliced

juice of 2 oranges

2 sprigs of thyme

1⅔ cups unsalted vegetable
   or chicken stock,
   or water

1½ ounces fresh spinach

Forget what those idiotic health fascists have to say about red meat. A young child needs it. This is stewed until it falls apart into wonderfully tender strands. Our old friend the sweet potato adds sweetness, as do the ubiquitous carrots.

Preheat the oven to 275°F. In an enamelled casserole, heat the butter with the oil and brown the meat in batches over a highish heat; remove the meat and set aside. Reduce the heat to medium.

Add the onions to the casserole and soften for about 5 minutes, then add the carrots, sweet potatoes, and mushrooms and cook for 5 minutes more. Return the meat to the pan and add the orange juice, thyme, and stock or water.

Bring to a boil, then cover the casserole and cook in the oven for 3 hours, or until the meat is tender. Add the spinach 15 minutes before the end of the cooking time.

Blitz until smooth, if necessary, to suit your child; adjust the consistency with boiled water if needed.

Spaghetti bollynaise

You can't fail with this classic, the mainstay of my youth. The real difference between this and my other version (see pages 165–167) is less salt and no booze. When my children were younger, I'd use the small stars rather than spaghetti, as they're easier to eat.

Heat the oil in a big saucepan over a medium heat and soften the onion for 5 minutes. Add the carrots, celery, and garlic and cook until soft, another 10 minutes. Turn up the heat, add the beef, and brown, stirring, for about 5 minutes.

Add the tomatoes, tomato purée, Worcestershire sauce, and stock. Bring to a boil, then simmer, covered, on a low heat for 30–40 minutes, stirring from time to time and breaking up the meat with a wooden spoon.

Boil the pasta following the package instructions. Blitz the sauce until smooth, if necessary, to suit your child, and serve with pasta and grated Parmesan.

{ MAKES 8 PORTIONS }

1 tablespoon olive oil
1 large onion, finely chopped
3 carrots, finely chopped
3 celery stalks, finely chopped
2 garlic cloves, finely chopped
1⅛ pounds ground beef
¾ pound tomatoes, peeled and
  chopped, or 1 (14.5-ounce)
  can chopped tomatoes
2 teaspoons tomato purée
1 tablespoon Worcestershire
  sauce
1¼ cups unsalted stock
  or water
pasta stars or spaghetti, to serve
freshly grated Parmesan,
  to serve

Chicken à la Lola

2 tablespoons unsalted butter
2 small onions, roughly chopped
2 large carrots, cut into
   small cubes
1 sweet potato, peeled and cut
   into small cubes
½ pound chicken breast (the
   best you can afford), cut into
   1-inch cubes
big handful of fresh spinach
mashed potato or cooked pasta,
   to serve

This was one of the first dishes I cooked for my daughter, Lola. It's packed with all sorts of worthy ingredients, and I added sweet potato (one tuber I've never really gotten the hang of) and carrot for an extra allure.

Melt the butter in a saucepan, add the onions, and soften over a medium heat for about 5 minutes.

Add the carrots and sweet potato and cook gently for another 5 minutes. Add the chicken and cook, stirring, until it is white.

Add 1 cup water, bring to a boil, then simmer, covered, for 20 minutes, or until the chicken is cooked through. Add the spinach and cook for 2–3 minutes more, until wilted.

Blitz until smooth, if necessary, to suit your child; adjust the consistency with boiled water if needed. For older children, just serve up as it is, with mashed potato or pasta.

Coriander chicken

I used to despise fresh coriander . . . literally couldn't look at the stuff. And, like the *Princess and the Pea*, I could detect even the tiniest leaf. This made Thai food a bore, and Indian, too. One day, though, I fell in love. Just like that. Now I couldn't live without its idiosyncratically metallic charms. I thought I'd try it out on Lola when she was young, to see what she thought. And she loved it. That said, at the age she is now, she declares love for one thing only to disown it the next day.

Melt the butter in a saucepan, add the onion, and soften over a medium heat for about 5 minutes.

Add the carrots and cook for 5 minutes more, then add the chicken and cook, stirring, until it is white. Add the coriander and watercress and cook for another minute.

Add the stock or water, bring to a boil, then turn down the heat and simmer, covered, for 20 minutes, or until the chicken is cooked through.

Blitz until smooth, if necessary, to suit your child; adjust the consistency with boiled water if needed.

{ MAKES 12 PORTIONS }

4 tablespoons unsalted butter
1 large onion, finely chopped
8 carrots, cut into small cubes
3 chicken breasts (the best you
  can afford), cut into 1-inch
  cubes
big handful of cilantro leaves,
  roughly chopped
big handful of watercress,
  roughly chopped
1⅔ cups unsalted stock
  or water

Chick 'n' carrots

{ **MAKES 8 PORTIONS** }

2 tablespoons unsalted butter

2 small onions, roughly chopped

7 carrots, cut into small cubes

2 chicken breasts (the best you
can afford), cut into 1-inch
cubes

3 ounces fresh spinach

1¼ cups unsalted stock
or water

Another chicken creation, with all sorts of goodness
hidden within.

Melt the butter in a saucepan, add the onions, and soften
over a medium heat for about 5 minutes.

Add the carrots and cook for another 5 minutes, then add
the chicken and cook, stirring, until it is white. Add the
spinach and cook for 2–3 minutes more, until wilted.

Add the stock or water, bring to a boil, then turn down
the heat and simmer, covered, for 20 minutes, or until the
chicken is cooked through.

Blitz until smooth, if necessary, to suit your child; adjust
the consistency with boiled water if needed.

Lola's favourite liver

OK, it doesn't sound too appetizing, but Lola used to adore this. And all that iron is a good thing. Bacon adds more flavour, as does sage.

Put the potatoes in a pan of cold water, bring to a boil, then simmer until soft, about 15 minutes. Drain, return to the pan, and leave to steam dry for 10 minutes. Mix in the butter and milk, then pass through a ricer and set aside. (Do not blitz the mashed potato in a blender or food processor or it will become like glue.)

Meanwhile, heat the oil in a frying pan over a medium heat, add the onion and bacon, and cook until the onion is soft and the bacon golden, about 5 minutes. Add the livers and fry for 2 minutes, until just browned. Add the sage and thyme, then ⅔ cup water, and simmer for 2 minutes, until the liver is cooked.

Blitz the liver mixture, if necessary, to suit your child, then mix with the mash.

{ MAKES 6 PORTIONS }

1⅔ pounds floury potatoes, peeled and cubed
2 tablespoons unsalted butter
2–3 tablespoons full-fat milk
1 tablespoon olive oil
1 small onion, finely chopped
3 rashers unsmoked back bacon, soaked in cold water for an hour to remove salt, and drained if making this for infants, then roughly chopped
½ pound chicken livers, cleaned and roughly chopped
4 sage leaves, roughly chopped
big pinch of thyme, roughly chopped

Fish pie jr

{ **MAKES 8 MINI PIES** }

2¼ pounds floury potatoes,
  peeled and cubed
1⅔ cups full-fat milk, plus
  2–3 tablespoons for the mash
11 tablespoons (1 stick plus
  3 tablespoons) unsalted butter
2 onions, roughly chopped
4 tomatoes, peeled, seeded,
  and roughly chopped
2 tablespoons all-purpose flour
1 pound cod fillet, skinned,
  pin-bones removed, cut into
  small chunks
1 pound salmon fillet,
  skinned, pin-bones removed,
  cut into small chunks
2 tablespoons finely chopped
  flat-leaf parsley
1 bay leaf
3½ ounces Cheddar, grated
1 egg, lightly beaten

I use salmon and cod for this, but you can substitute haddock, pollack, or whatever. As the children get older, I tend to add good smoked haddock, too.

Put the potatoes in a pan of cold water, bring to a boil, then simmer until soft, about 15 minutes. Drain, add 2–3 tablespoons milk and half the butter, and mash until it is smooth.

Preheat the oven to 350°F.

Melt the remaining the butter in a heavy-based pan over a medium heat and soften the onions for 5 minutes. Add the tomatoes and cook for another couple of minutes, then stir in the flour and cook for 1 minute more.

Add the milk, bring to a boil, and cook, stirring, for 1 minute. Then add the fish, parsley, and bay leaf and simmer for 5 minutes, stirring from time to time, until the fish is just cooked. Remove the bay leaf, add the cheese, and stir until melted.

Divide the fish mixture among 8 ramekins, top with mashed potato, and brush with beaten egg. Bake for 15–20 minutes until the potato is golden and the fish mixture is bubbling and piping-hot.

Salmon with carrots & tomatoes

Buy the best farmed salmon you can afford. It keeps well in the freezer. Cheese adds more flavour, as the fish can tend towards the bland. Do make sure you remove any errant bones.

Steam the carrots for 15 minutes.

Meanwhile, put the salmon in a saucepan, cover with the milk, and simmer gently for 6 minutes until cooked. Drain and set aside, reserving the milk.

Melt the butter in a pan over a low heat, add the tomatoes, and cook until mushy. Add the cheese and cook until melted, then blitz with the carrots until you have a coarse mash. Flake the fish and add to the tomato and cheese mixture.

Blitz until smooth if necessary to suit your child; adjust the consistency with some of the reserved poaching milk if needed.

{ MAKES 8 PORTIONS }

6 carrots, cut into small cubes
⅔ pound salmon fillet, skinned and pin-bones removed
scant 1 cup full-fat milk
3 tablespoons unsalted butter
4 ripe tomatoes, peeled, seeded, and roughly chopped
3½ ounces Cheddar, grated

Fishcakes

{ MAKES 16 SMALL OR
  8 LARGE FISHCAKES }

⅔ pound cod, skinned
  and pin-bones removed
⅔ pound salmon, skinned
  and pin-bones removed
1¼ cups full-fat milk
3 rashers unsmoked back bacon,
  soaked in cold water for an
  hour to remove salt and
  drained if making this for
  infants
1⅓ pounds floury potatoes,
  peeled and cubed
1 tablespoon unsalted butter
2 teaspoons tomato ketchup
1 teaspoon English mustard
2 tablespoons flat-leaf parsley,
  finely chopped
freshly ground black pepper
all-purpose flour, for dusting
2–4 tablespoons olive oil

Lots of fishy goodness packed in here, with the bacon adding a touch of depth and smoke. The children both gobble up every last morsel. A rare sight indeed.

Put the fish in a pan, add the milk, and poach for 4 minutes. Drain and flake the fish, reserving the milk. Set aside.

Fry the bacon until crisp; chop into small pieces, and set aside.

Put the potatoes in a pan of cold water, bring to a boil, then simmer until soft, about 15 minutes. Drain, return to the pan, and leave to steam dry for 10 minutes. Mix in the butter and a good splash of the reserved poaching milk, then pass through a ricer and set aside.

Mix the mashed potato with the fish, bacon, ketchup, mustard, parsley, and pepper.

Shape into small balls, flatten, then leave to rest in the fridge, covered, for 1 hour on a baking sheet.

Dust the fishcakes very lightly with flour. Heat a little olive oil in a frying pan over a high heat and fry the fishcakes in batches until crisp and golden and cooked through.

Cheesy pasta

This really is an emergency fallback, needing just pasta, butter, Parmesan, and Cheddar. If you're lacking one cheese, use more of the other.

Cook the pasta as directed on the package. Drain.

Melt the butter on the hot pasta and add the cheeses, mixing quite hard. Add pepper and serve immediately.

{ **SERVES 2** }

3 ounces baby pasta or spaghetti
3 tablespoons unsalted butter
handful of grated Parmesan
handful of grated Cheddar
freshly ground black pepper

Tomato & veg pasta sauce

{ MAKES 10 PORTIONS }

4 medium carrots, sliced
1 pound cauliflower, cut into
 florets, woody core discarded
7 tablespoons (¾ stick plus
 1 tablespoon) unsalted butter
2¼ pounds tomatoes, peeled,
 seeded, and roughly chopped
7 ounces Cheddar, grated
baby pasta, to serve

Full of carefully hidden vegetables.

Steam the carrots and cauliflower for 7 minutes.

Melt the butter in a saucepan, add the tomatoes, and cook over a medium heat for 5 minutes. Add the cheese and stir until melted. Boil the pasta following the package instructions and drain.

Blitz the tomato and cheese mixture with the veg. Serve with the pasta.

Lentil salad

It's bad enough trying to force lentils down the throats of grown men, let alone squealing children. But lentils, cooked well (i.e. not into a muddy mush) are a noble ingredient: cheap, easy to store, and possessed of a wonderfully nutty, earthy taste. I particularly like those tiny greenish-brown ones from Puy in France, but most are OK. Wash first, to remove any unwelcome stones and twigs, then cook at a simmer for anything from 25 minutes to an hour. You want them al dente. This recipe was born in Sicily when I was cooking for about eight children. They were bored with pasta, as we'd had the stuff day in and day out for the past two weeks. So I just gathered together what was close to hand. For adults, add chilli and more salt.

{ SERVES 8 }

1 pound Puy lentils, rinsed

1 onion, halved, plus 2 onions, finely chopped

1 garlic clove, peeled, plus 2–3 garlic cloves, finely chopped

2 bay leaves

2 tablespoons olive oil, plus 4 tablespoons extra-virgin olive oil for the dressing

¾ pound tomatoes, peeled, seeded, and chopped

big handful of flat-leaf parsley, finely chopped

sea salt and freshly ground black pepper

2–3 tablespoons white wine vinegar

Put the lentils in a big saucepan along with the halved onion, whole garlic clove, and the bay leaves. (Do not salt the water, as this can make the skins tough.) Bring to a boil, then reduce to a simmer; the lentils may take anything from 25–60 minutes, so keep tasting; they're done when they're still firm, but with a little give. Drain, remove the onion, garlic, and bay leaves, and set aside.

Heat 2 tablespoons of the olive oil in a frying pan and soften the chopped onions and garlic over a medium heat for 10 minutes, then mix with lentils.

Add the tomatoes and parsley to the lentils and mix, then season to taste (you'll need salt unless cooking for very young children), and throw in the remaining olive oil and vinegar. Serve.

Lunch from a late summer English garden

{ MAKES 8 PORTIONS }

2 chicken breasts (the best you
    can afford), cut into small dice
juice of 1 lime
2 teaspoons honey
a splash of low-sodium
    soy sauce
2 tablespoons unsalted butter
1 tablespoon olive oil
4 small red onions,
    finely chopped
6 small courgettes, diced
4 small carrots, diced
8 rashers unsmoked streaky
    bacon or pancetta, soaked
    in cold water for an hour to
    remove salt and drained if
    making this for infants, diced
1¼ cups low-sodium chicken
    stock or water
freshly ground black pepper
boiled rice or new potatoes,
    to serve

Every August we go down to my mother's house in the country for a week or so. If the weather's good, life's good. Less so if it's dreary and drizzling. My mother's kitchen garden, though, is incredible. One day, I walked through with a basket, picking whatever looked good—tiny red onions, elegant carrots, baby courgettes, and endless herbs.

Put the chicken in a bowl, add the lime juice, honey, and soy sauce, cover, and marinate in the fridge for 2 hours.

Melt the butter and oil in a big saucepan, add the onions, and soften over a low to medium heat for about 5 minutes. Add the courgettes and carrots. Increase the heat to medium-high, add the bacon, and fry until just crisp, then reduce the heat, add the chicken, reserving the marinade, and cook for 5 minutes.

Add the reserved marinade, stock or water, a little pepper to taste, and simmer for 10 minutes more, or until the chicken is cooked through. Serve with boiled rice or new potatoes.

Red sauce for pasta

There's always some of this sauce in the deep freeze, and when supplies start to dwindle, the only work involved is chopping a few onions and cloves of garlic. As for the basil, I bought a plant in Tesco a year back, repotted it, and it sits at the kitchen window, flourishing.

Heat the oil in a big saucepan over a low to medium heat and soften the onion and garlic for 10 minutes.

Add the tomato purée and cook for a minute, then add the tomatoes and sugar and stir. Add a generous grinding of black pepper, then simmer gently for 40 minutes, stirring from time to time, until thickened.

Boil the pasta following the package instructions.

Remove the sauce from the heat and stir in the basil and Parmesan. Serve with the pasta.

{ MAKES 16 PORTIONS }

2 tablespoons olive oil
1 large onion, finely chopped
2 garlic cloves, finely chopped
2 teaspoons tomato purée
1¾ pounds tomatoes, peeled, seeded, and chopped, or 1 (28-ounce) can chopped tomatoes
pinch of superfine sugar
freshly ground black pepper
handful of basil, roughly chopped
handful of grated Parmesan
pasta or baby pasta, to serve

Veggie mess

{ MAKES 6 PORTIONS }

2 sweet potatoes, peeled and
   cut into ½-inch cubes

8 carrots, sliced

1 cauliflower, cut into florets,
   woody core discarded

1½ ounces fresh spinach

This purée has a good flavour and is, of course, packed with
veggie goodness.

Steam the sweet potatoes and carrots for 10 minutes, then
blitz until smooth; adjust the consistency with boiled water,
if needed, and set aside.

Steam the cauliflower for 10 minutes, adding the spinach
for the last 2 minutes. Blitz until smooth; again, adjust the
consistency with boiled water if needed. Add to the sweet
potato and carrot purée and mix to combine.

Cupcakes

I can't bear these gaudy, oversweet confections, and this
is one craze that has entirely passed me by. My daughter,
though, disagrees and is obsessed with the things. So we
spent an afternoon making the cake batter, baking, then
decorating, and she was in utter heaven. I enjoyed myself,
too, and it's become a regular, if messy, way to spend a
wet Saturday afternoon. I've gone for a pink-tinted white
chocolate icing, but you can use any colour you like. As for
decorations—edible silver balls, sprinkles, Smarties, Rolos,
edible glitter—the choice is relentless.

Preheat the oven to 350°F. Line a 12-well cupcake pan with
paper liners.

Put the flour, cocoa powder, superfine sugar, and butter into
a food processor and blend until mixed. Add half the milk
and blend briefly to mix.

In a bowl, whisk the remaining milk with the egg and
vanilla extract. Beat for 30 seconds, then pour into the flour
mixture and blend until just smooth; do not overmix.

Spoon into the lined cupcake pan, filling each well about
two-thirds full. Bake for 15–20 minutes, until pale golden
and the cakes spring back when you touch them lightly.
Allow to cool on a wire rack.

For the icing, mix the butter and confectioners' sugar in a
food processor until smooth. Transfer to a bowl and
gradually fold in the melted chocolate (it should be barely
warm), vanilla seeds, and food colouring. Cool in the fridge
for 20–30 minutes.

Using an pastry bag or palette knife, cover the cakes
with icing. Decorate—or let your children take over.
Leave to set.

{ MAKES 12 }

¾ cup self-rising flour, sifted
¼ cup cocoa powder, sifted
⅔ cup plus 1 tablespoon
   superfine sugar
3 tablespoons unsalted butter,
   at room temperature
½ cup full-fat milk
1 large egg
½ teaspoon vanilla extract
edible glitter, sprinkles,
   chocolate buttons, Smarties,
   etc., to decorate

For the icing

9 tablespoons (1 stick plus
   1 tablespoon) butter, at
   room temperature
1 cup confectioners' sugar, sifted
4½ ounces white chocolate,
   melted
seeds scraped from ½ vanilla
   bean
1 drop pink food colouring
   (or any colour you fancy)

Chocolate chip cookies

{ MAKES 12–15 }

8 tablespoons (1 stick) unsalted
  butter, softened, plus extra for
  greasing
⅓ cup superfine sugar
1 medium egg yolk
2 drops vanilla extract
1 cup plus 2 tablespoons
  all-purpose flour, sifted
¼–⅓ cup chocolate chips, either
  posh chocolate or something
  good such as Dairy Milk,
  smashed into pieces

This is a recipe from Caroline, my mother-in-law, and it's
a cracker. The cookies are so easy that Lola can bake them.
Usually rather better than I.

Preheat the oven to 350°F. Grease a large baking sheet
with butter.

In a large bowl, cream the butter, sugar, egg yolk, and
vanilla extract with a wooden spoon.

Add the flour gradually, stirring to make thick dough.
Then stir in the chocolate chips.

Scoop out a dessertspoon of dough at a time, mold into a
ball, and place on the greased baking sheet. Press with your
fingertips to flatten into cookie shapes. Leave plenty of
space between each cookie.

Bake for 12–15 minutes, until lightly golden but still a little
soft in the middle. Let them cool a little before eating.
Easier said than done.

Index

Acknowledgments

I'd like to thank the following, for their help, support, advice, recipes, photographs, design, and inspiration: Cristian Barnett, Alex Bilmes, Luca del Bono, Caroline Buys, Antonio Carluccio, Richard Corrigan, Anne Dolamore, Ben Elliot, Alberto Figueroa, Matthew Fort, Gerard Greaves, Geordie Greig, Georgie Hewitt, Nigel Haworth, Fergus Henderson, Mark Hix, Simon Hopkinson, Reg Johnson, Sam Joiner, Bill Knott, Jeremy Lee, Sebastian Lee, Giorgio Locatelli, Laura Lopes, Justine Pattison, Polly Powell, Maggie Ramsay, Allan Sommerville, David Thompson, Ewan Venters, and Fran Warde. As well as my mother and father; Grainne Fox, my ever-brilliant agent, and Becca Spry, who guided, edited, and nurtured this book with a truly expert, elegant hand. And last of all to Sara, who continues to taste all the recipes with gilded palate and stoic expertise. As well as continuing to put up with me.

Favourite suppliers

Some of my favorite online suppliers in the UK are **The Blackface Meat Company** and **Ginger Pig** for lamb, veal, venison, and feathered game, and rare breed pork, lamb, and beef in turn. I also love **Japanese Kitchen** for dried noodles, miso paste, and other Eastern delicacies, and **Lakeland**, a British institution, for everything you need for your kitchen and a lot more you don't, but covet all the same.

But practicality and frugality are part of the charm of the weekday meals in this book, and I don't want you to be slammed with shipping charges and vexatious price conversions when you're shopping for ingredients. Here's a list of places I like in the United States and Canada:

D'Artagnan www.dartagnan.com
For sausages, cured and smoked meats, duck, and game birds.

Ottomanelli's www.nycotto.com
Beef, lamb, veal, and poultry from a legendary New York City butcher.

J. Willy Krauch & Sons www.willykrauch.com
Smoked, when available.

Penzeys www.penzeys.com
Midwestern (Wauwatosa, Wisconsin) emporium for over 250 spices, herbs, specialty ingredients, and an excellent selection of chillies to use in the recipes in this book.

Asian Food Grocer www.asianfoodgrocer.com
Mirin, miso paste, dried noodles, short and long grain rice, toothsome Japanese snacks, and more.

Russ & Daughters www.russanddaughters.com
Caviar and smoked fish in glorious abundance.

Bridge Kitchenware www.bridgekitchenware.com
Professional cookware, specialty tools, and an emporium's worth of other culinary equipment.